AF342584

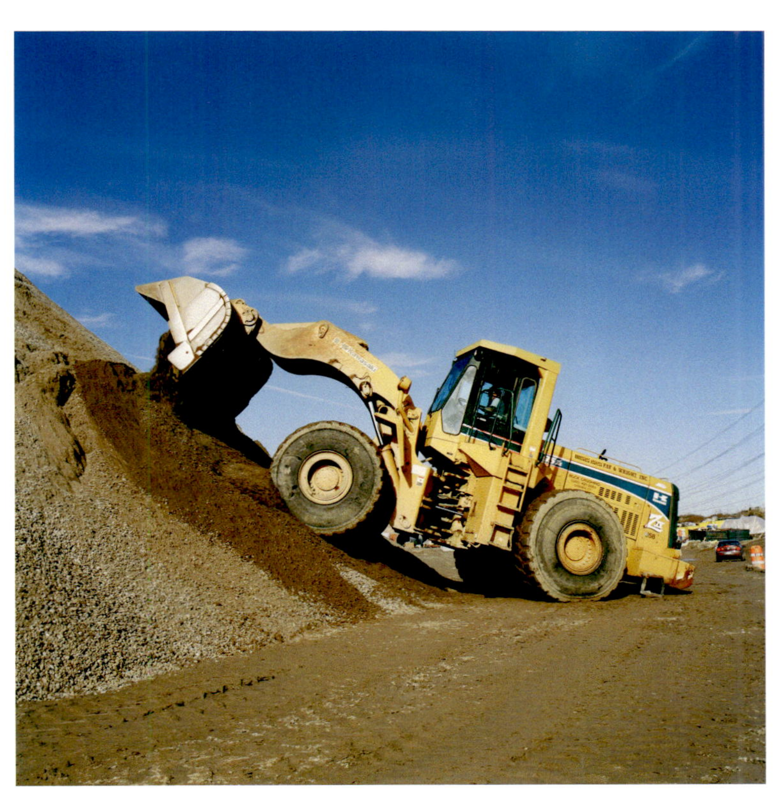

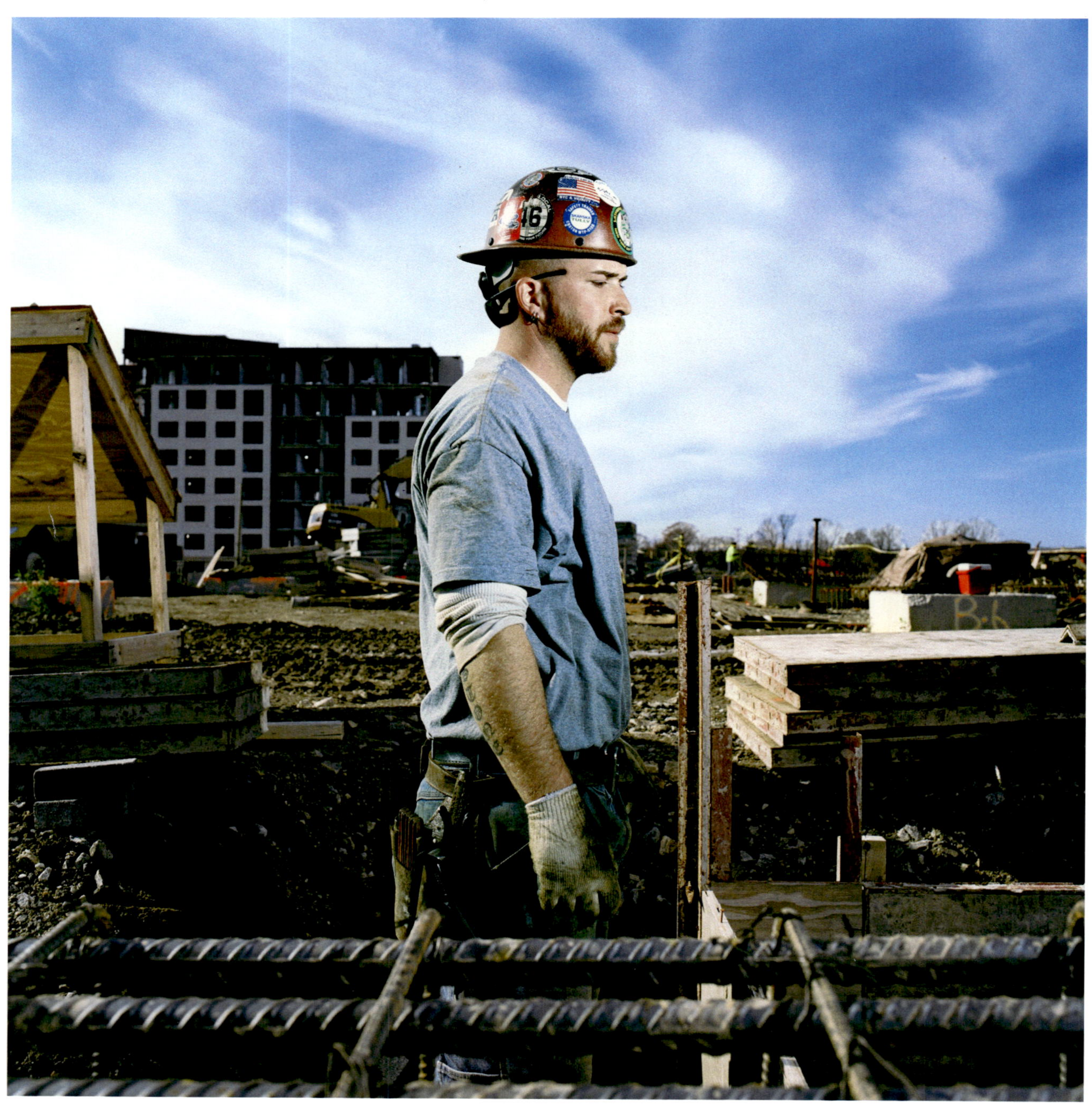

CONSTRUCTION

BRIAN FINKE

ESSAY BY WHITNEY JOHNSON

DECODE BOOKS

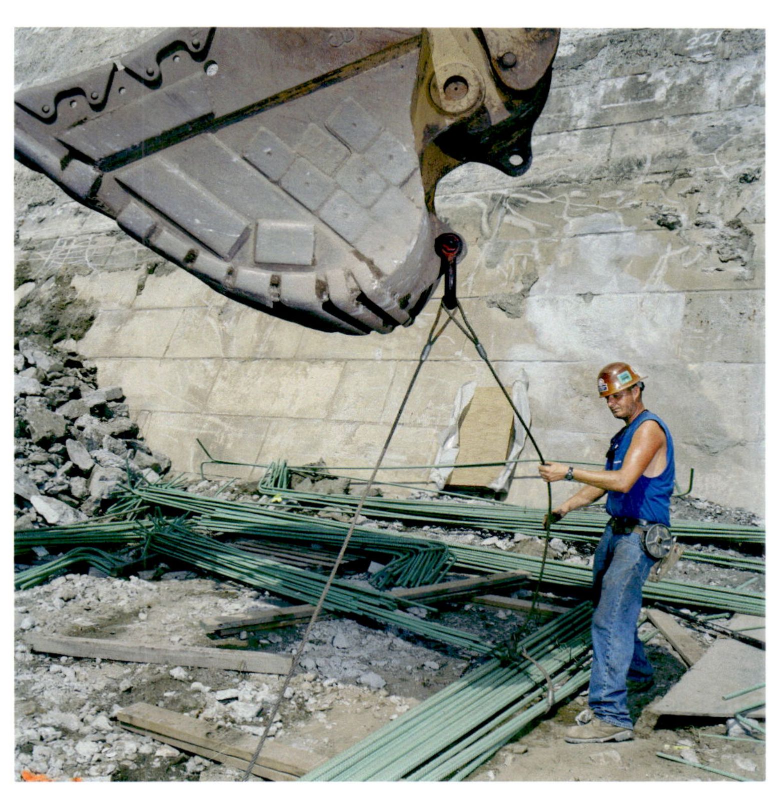

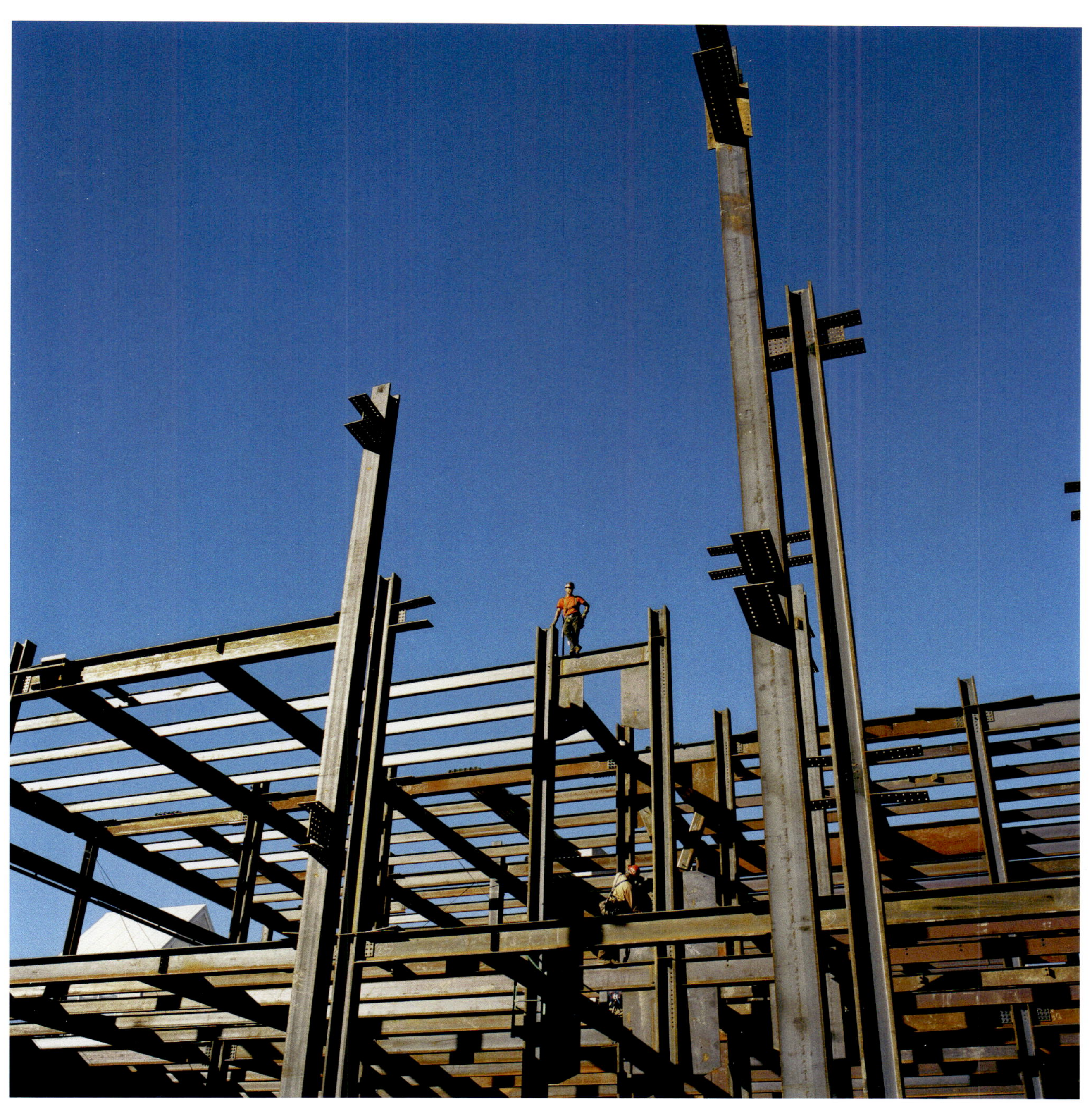

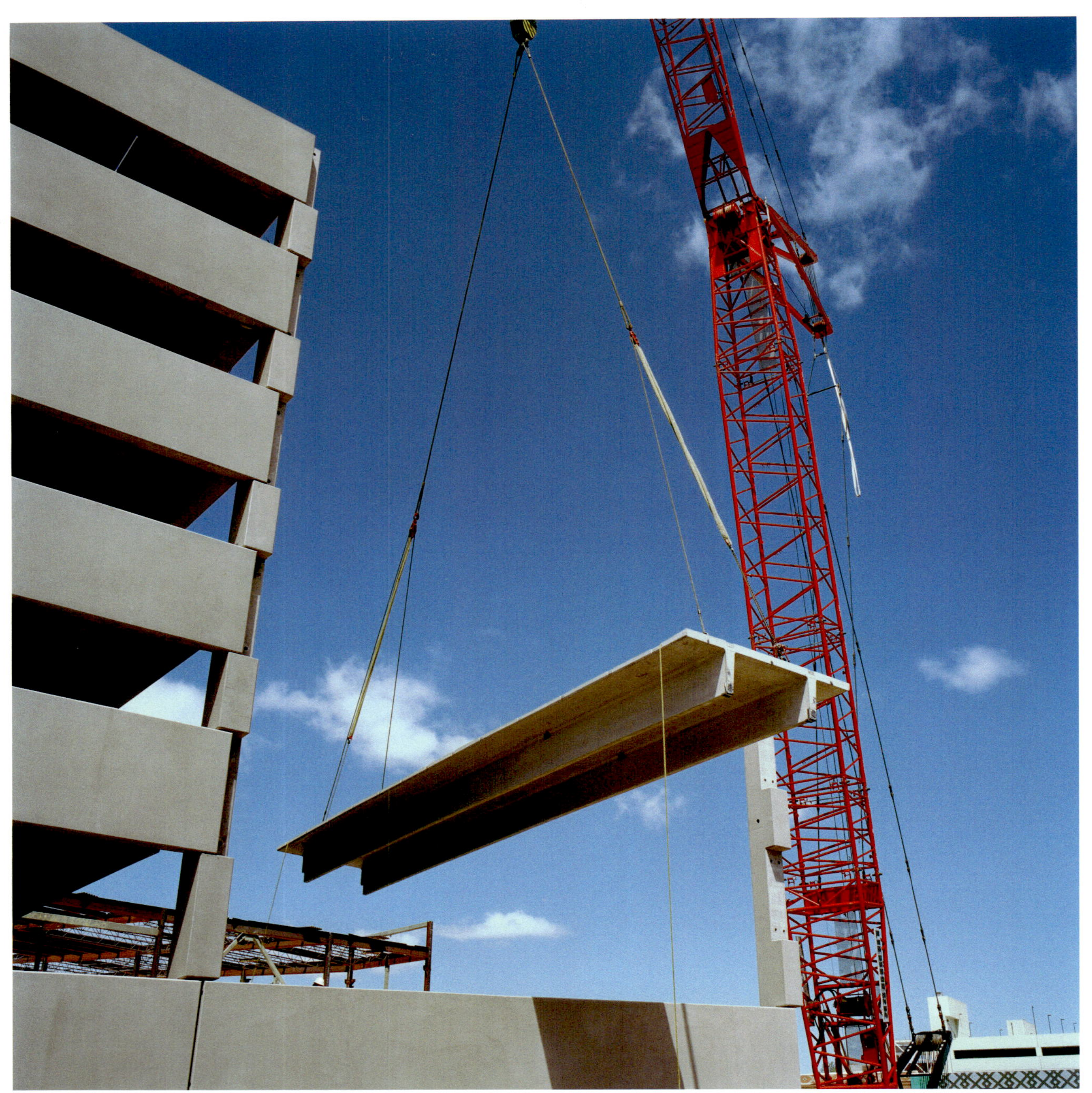

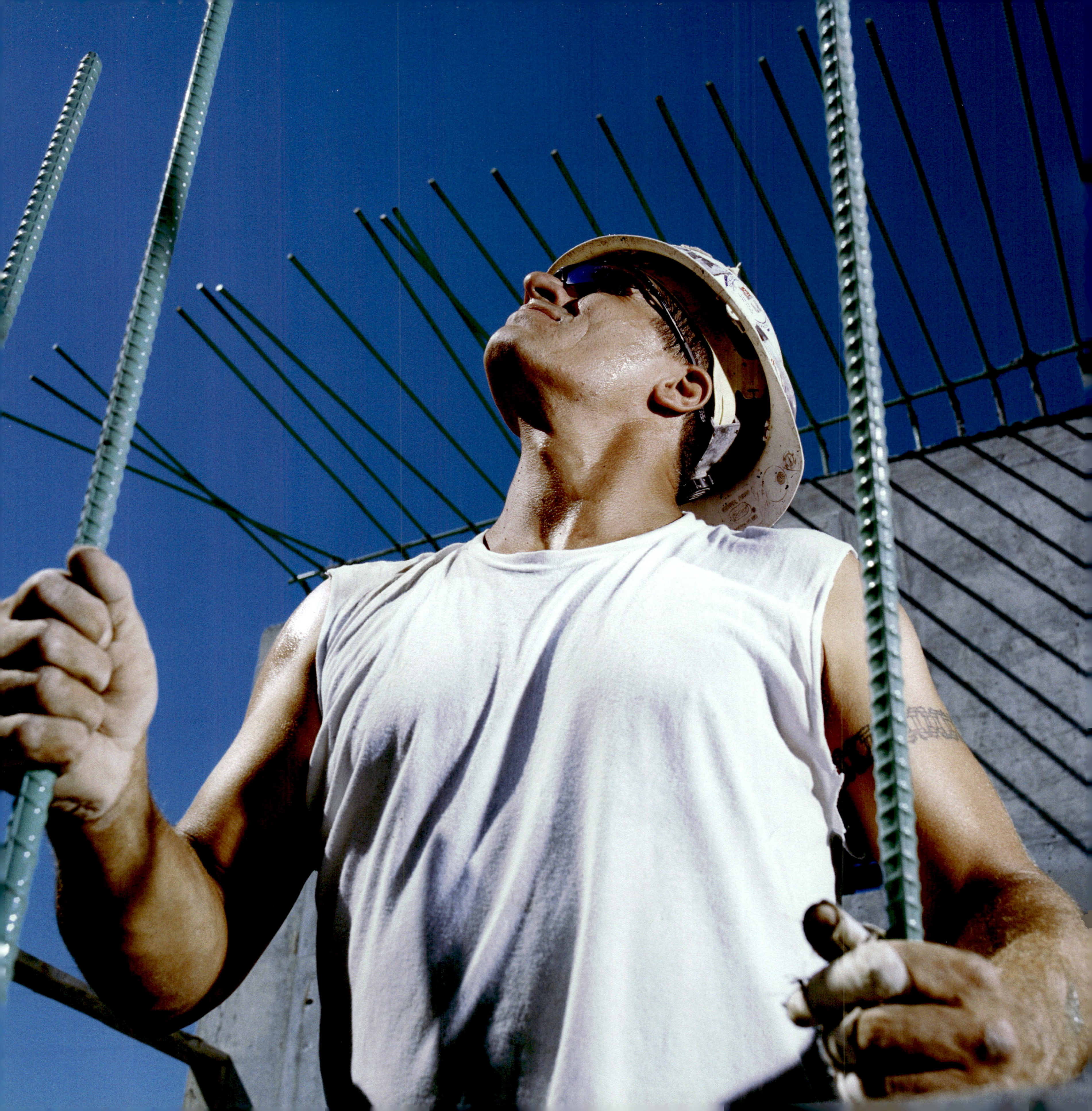

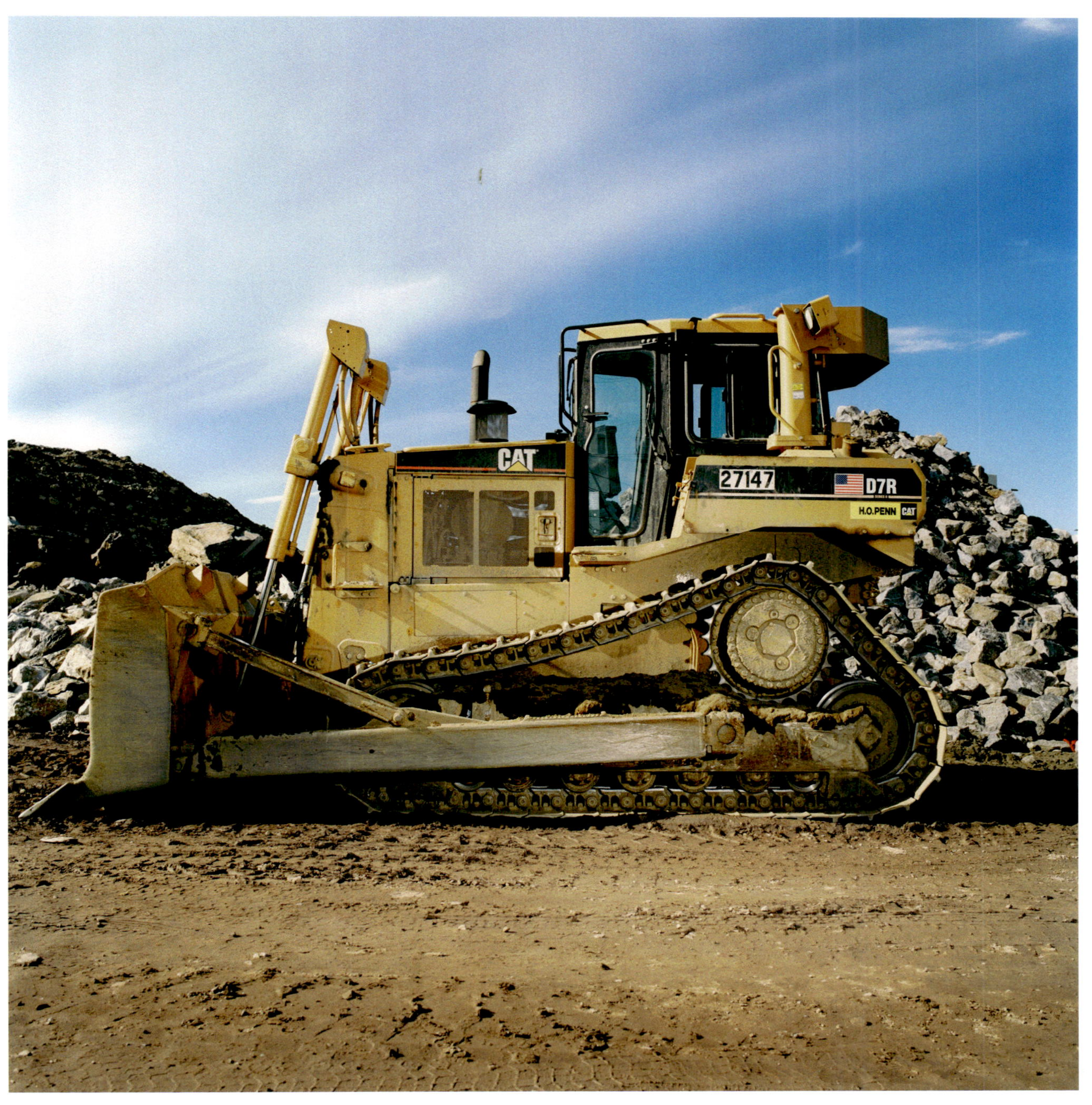
CAT
27147
D7R
H.O.PENN CAT

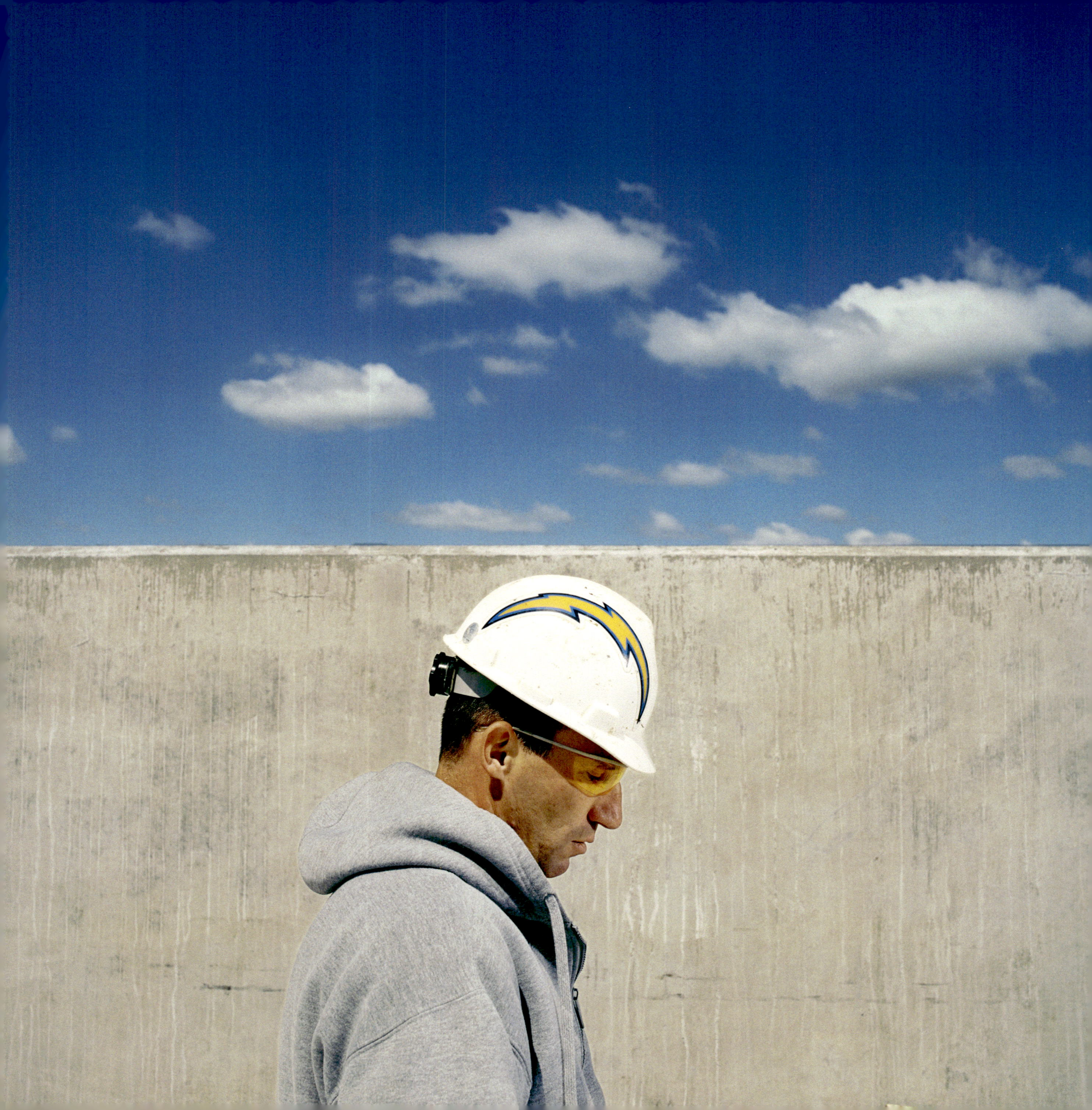

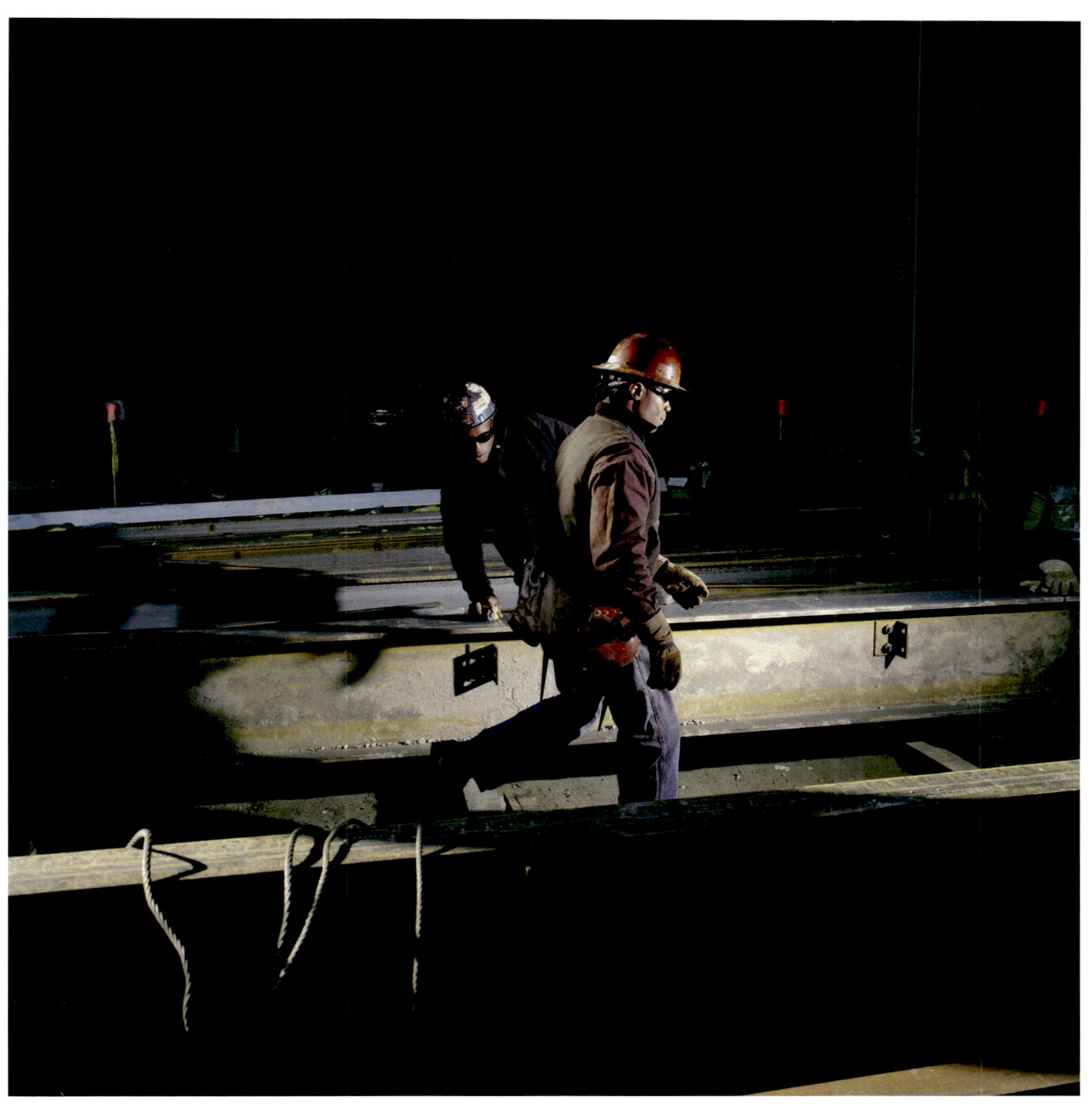

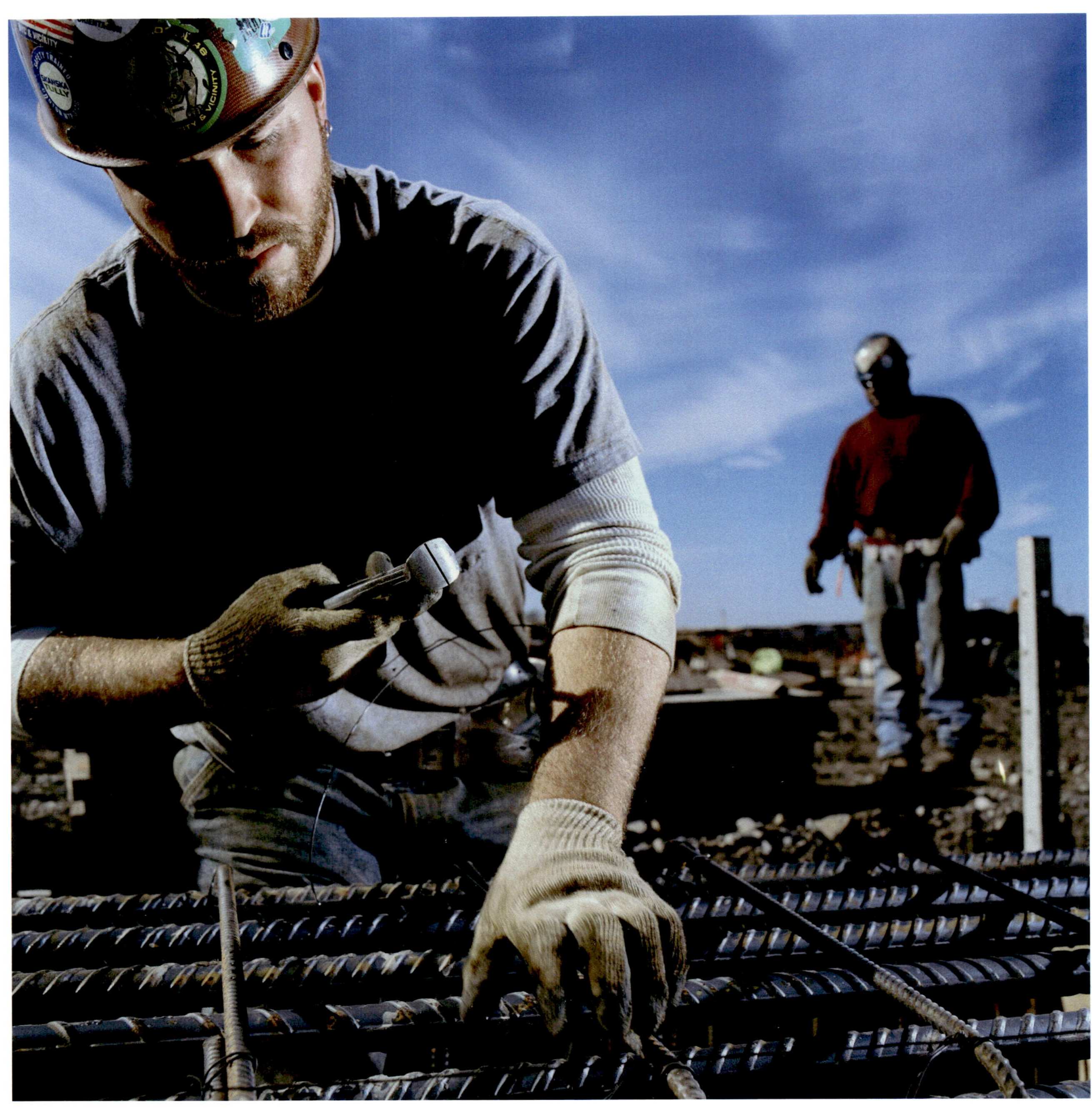

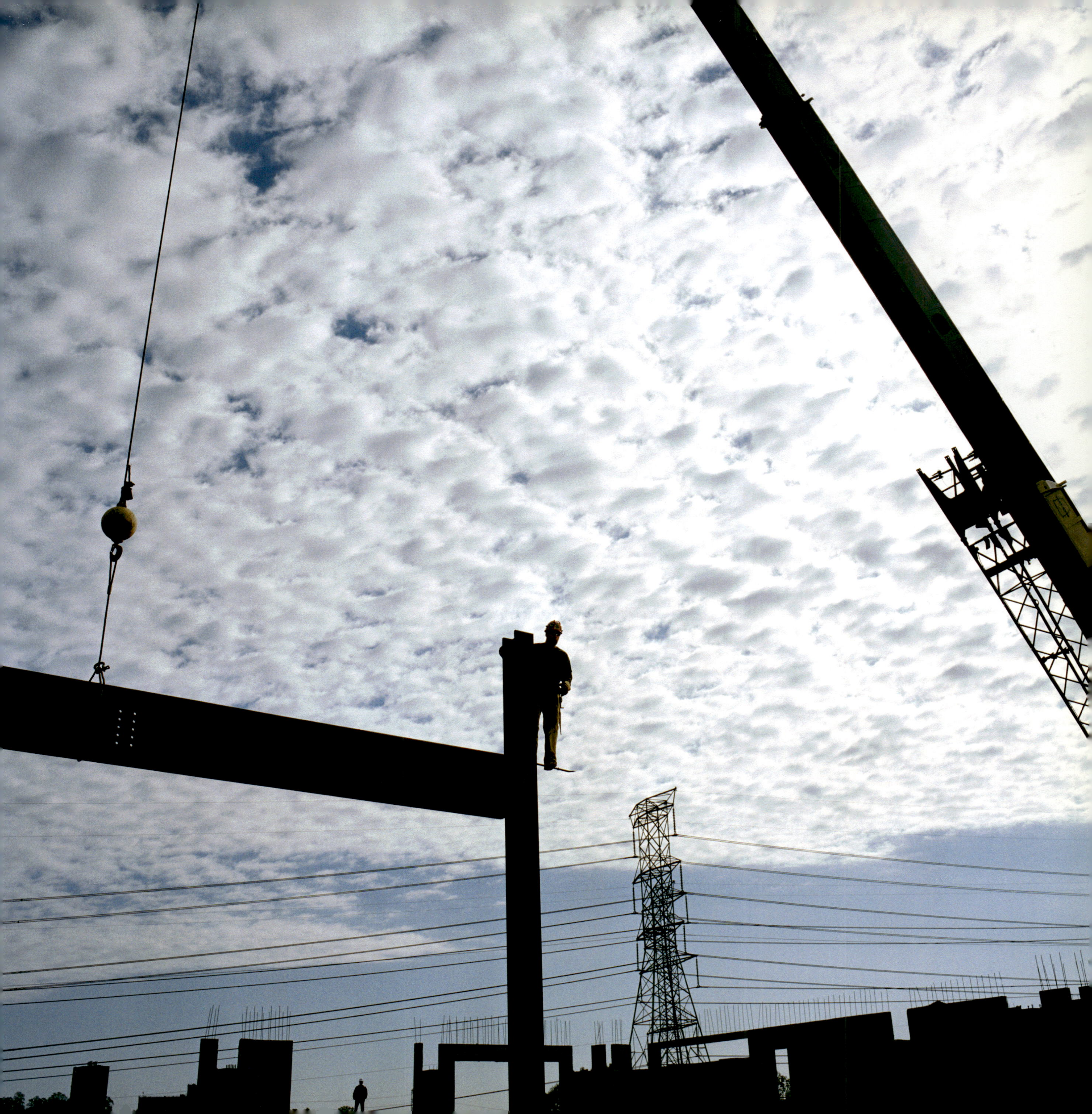

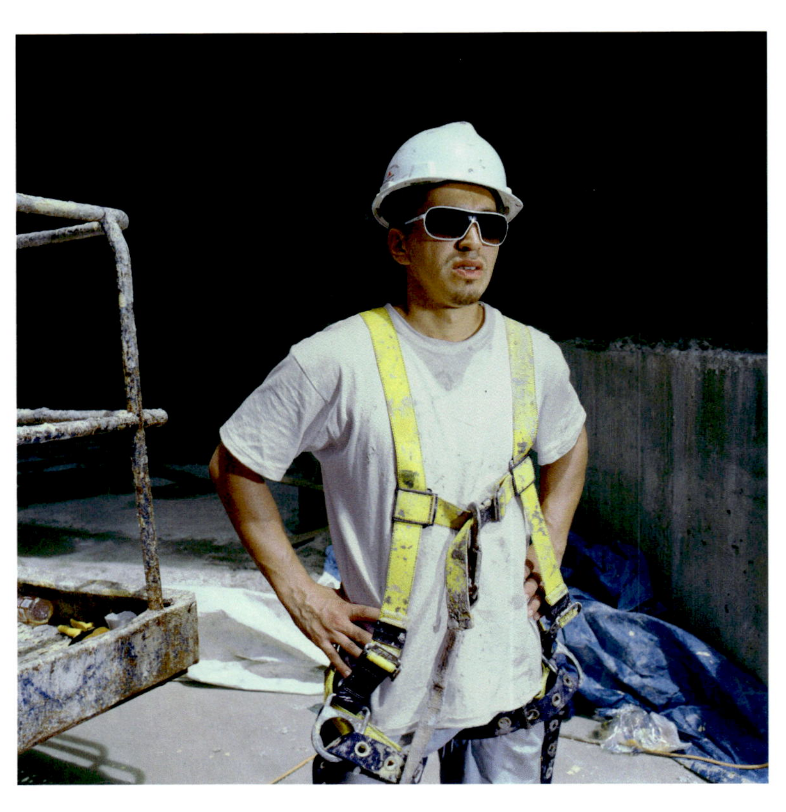
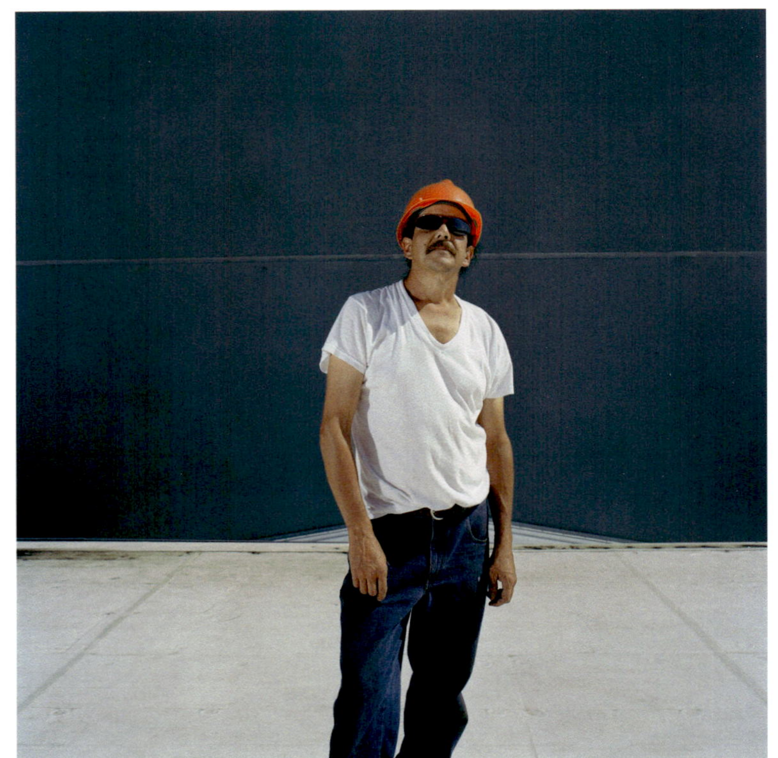

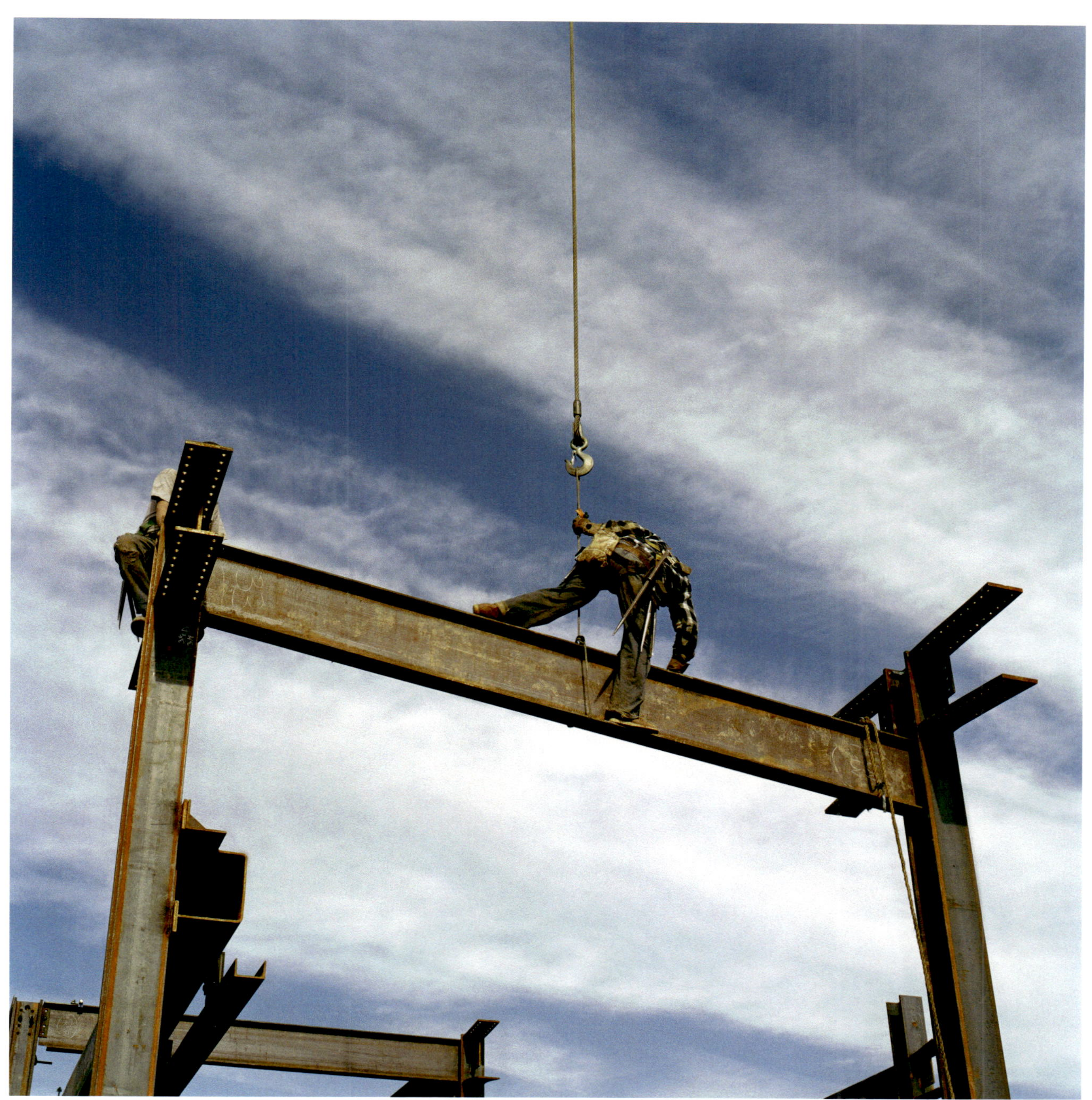

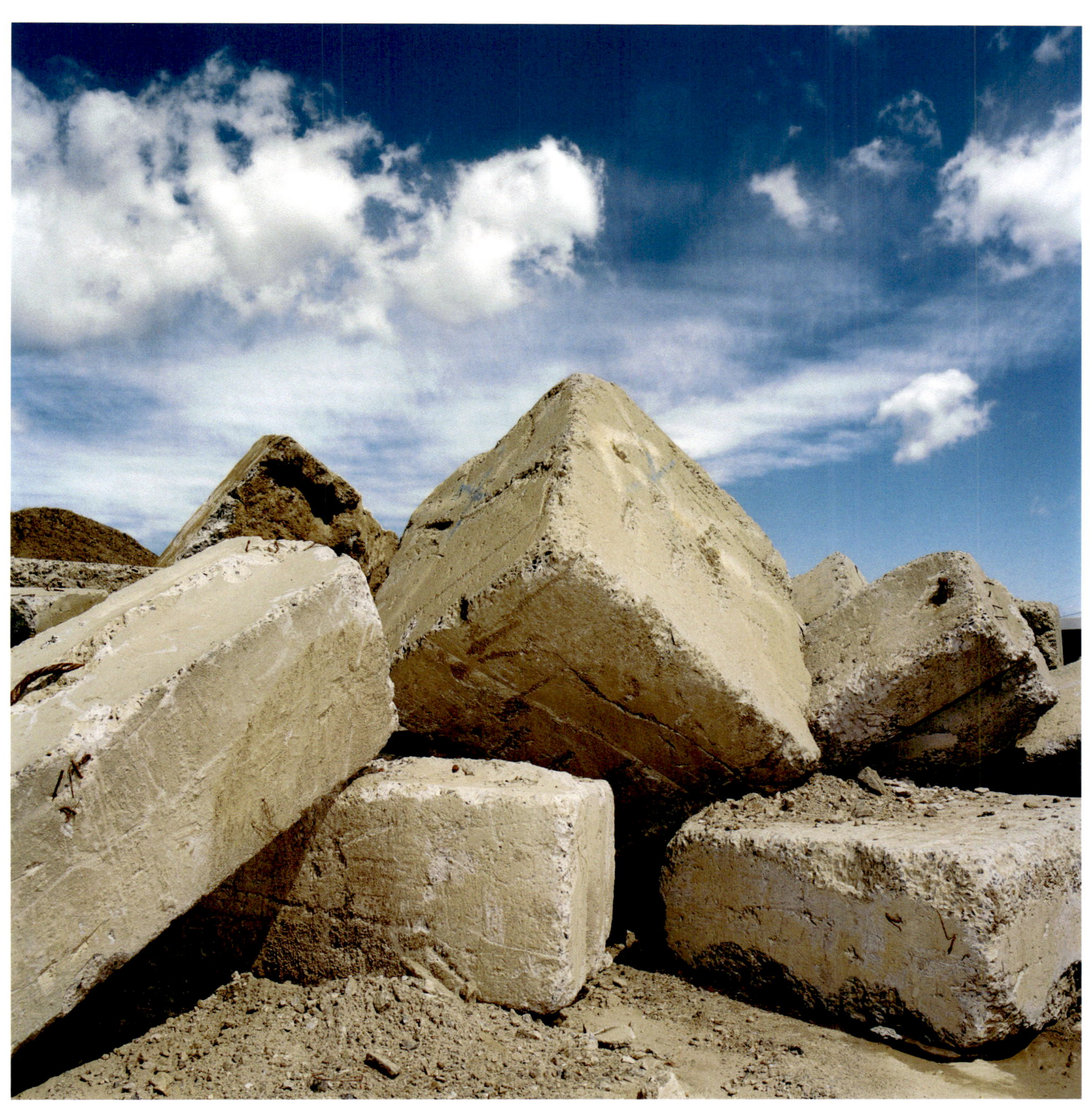

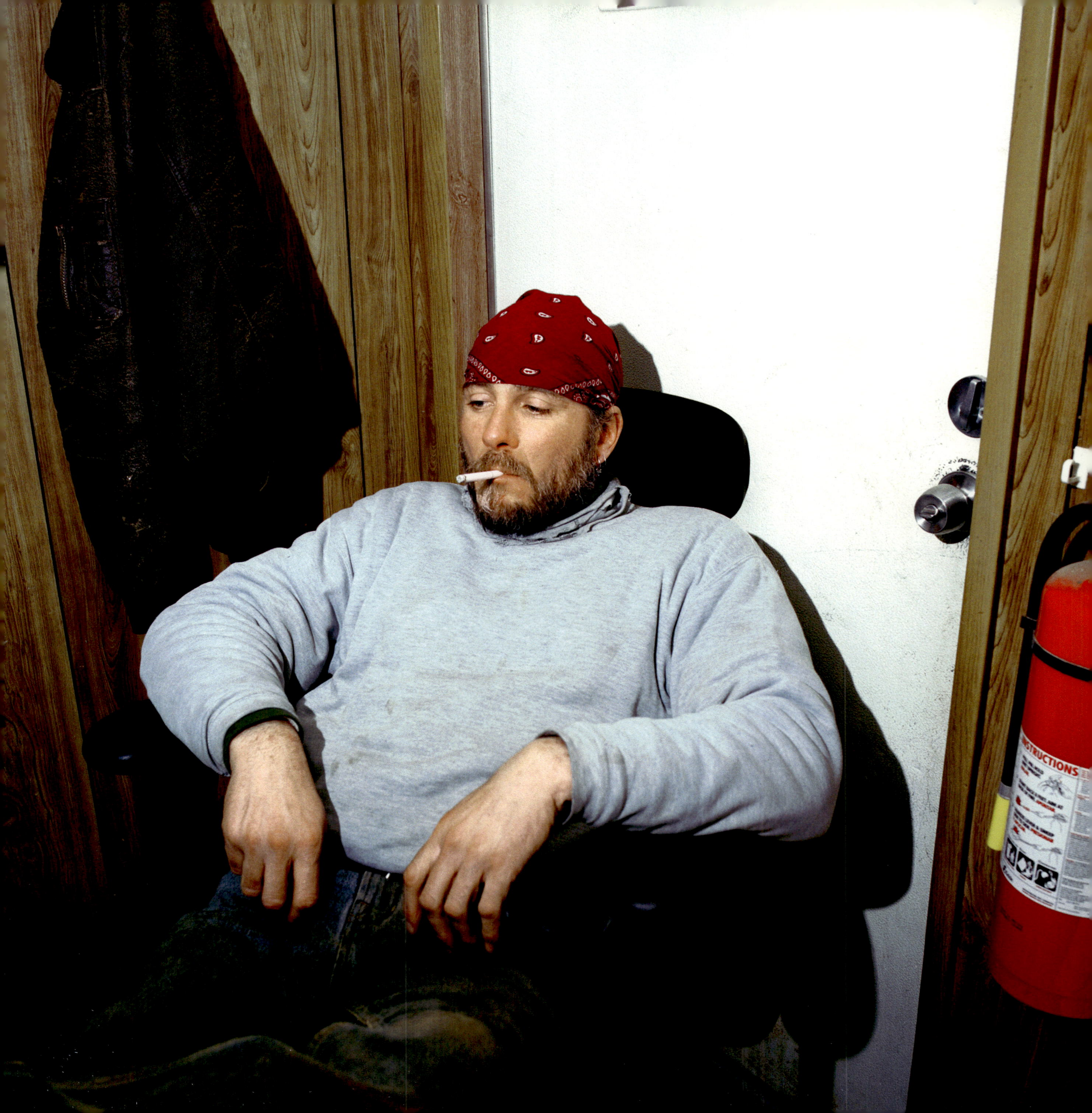

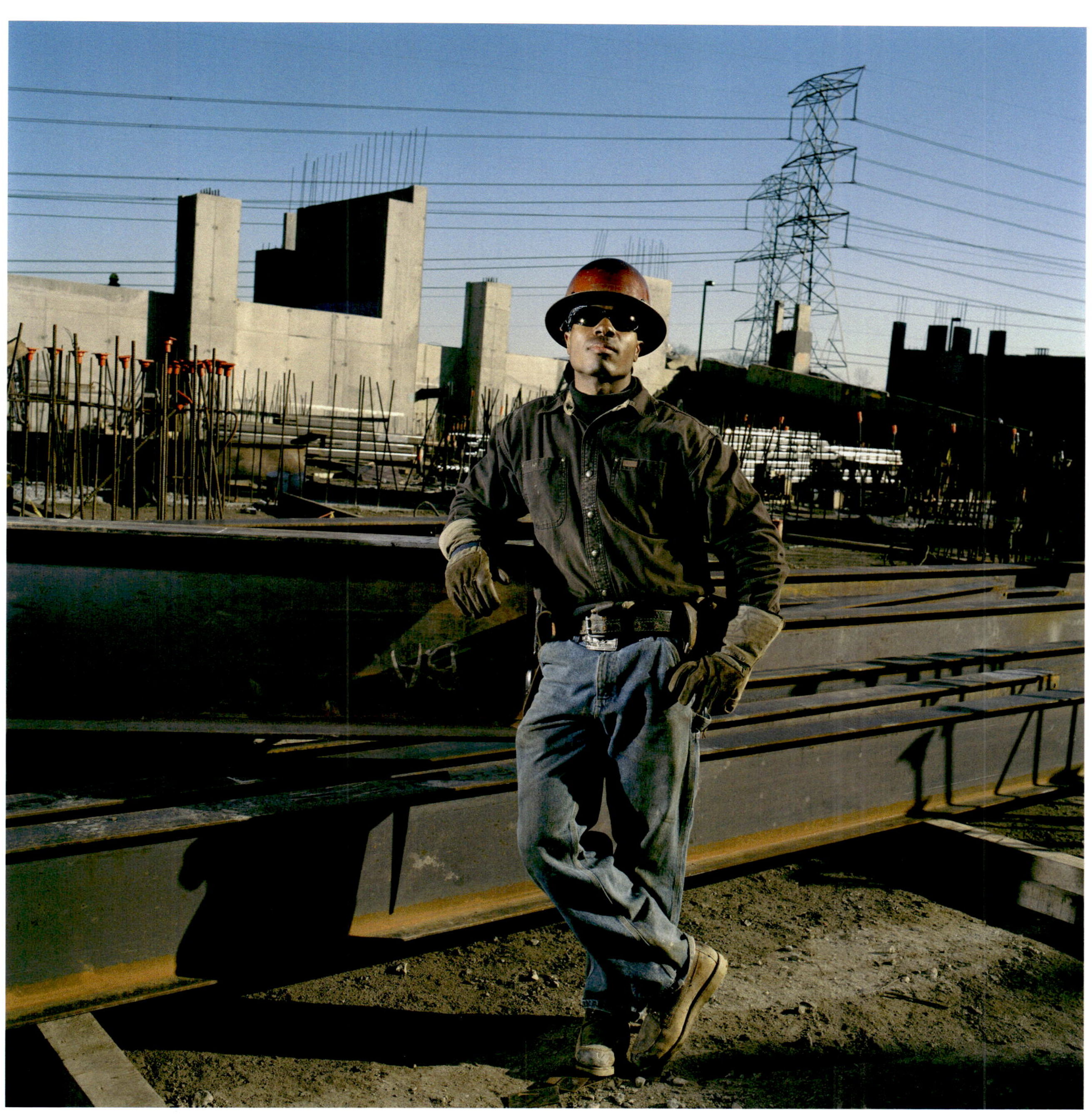

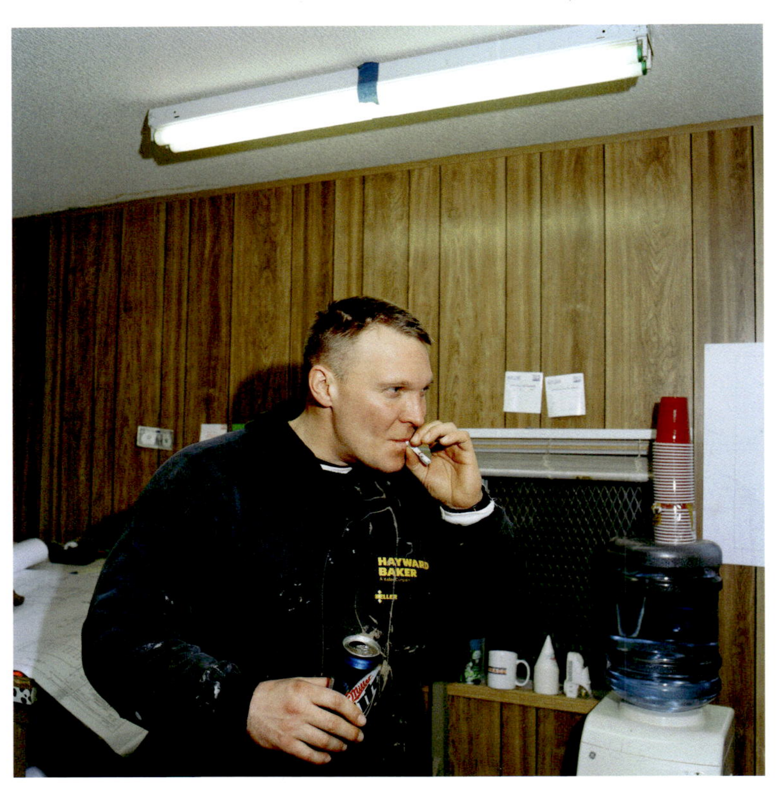
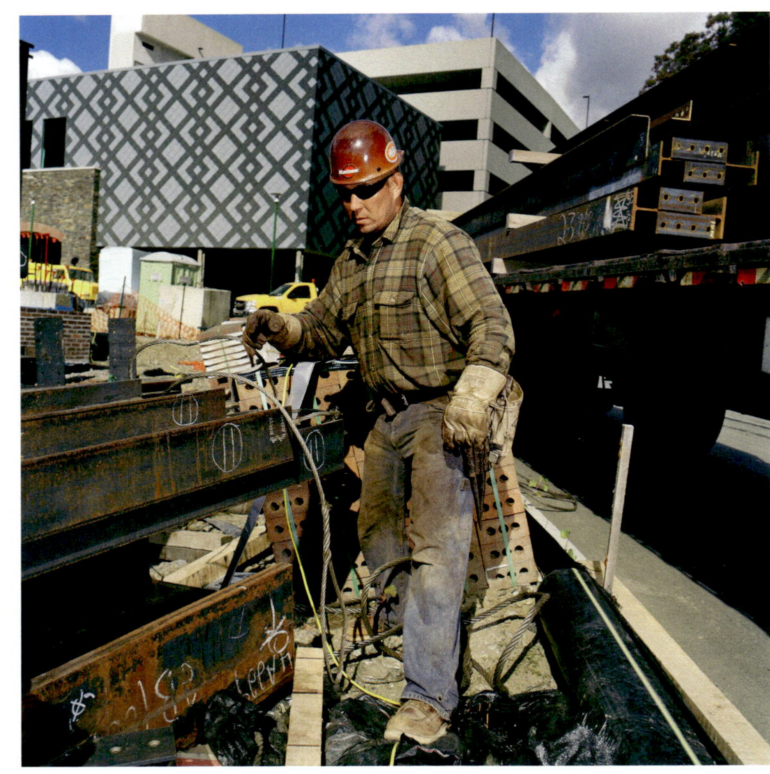

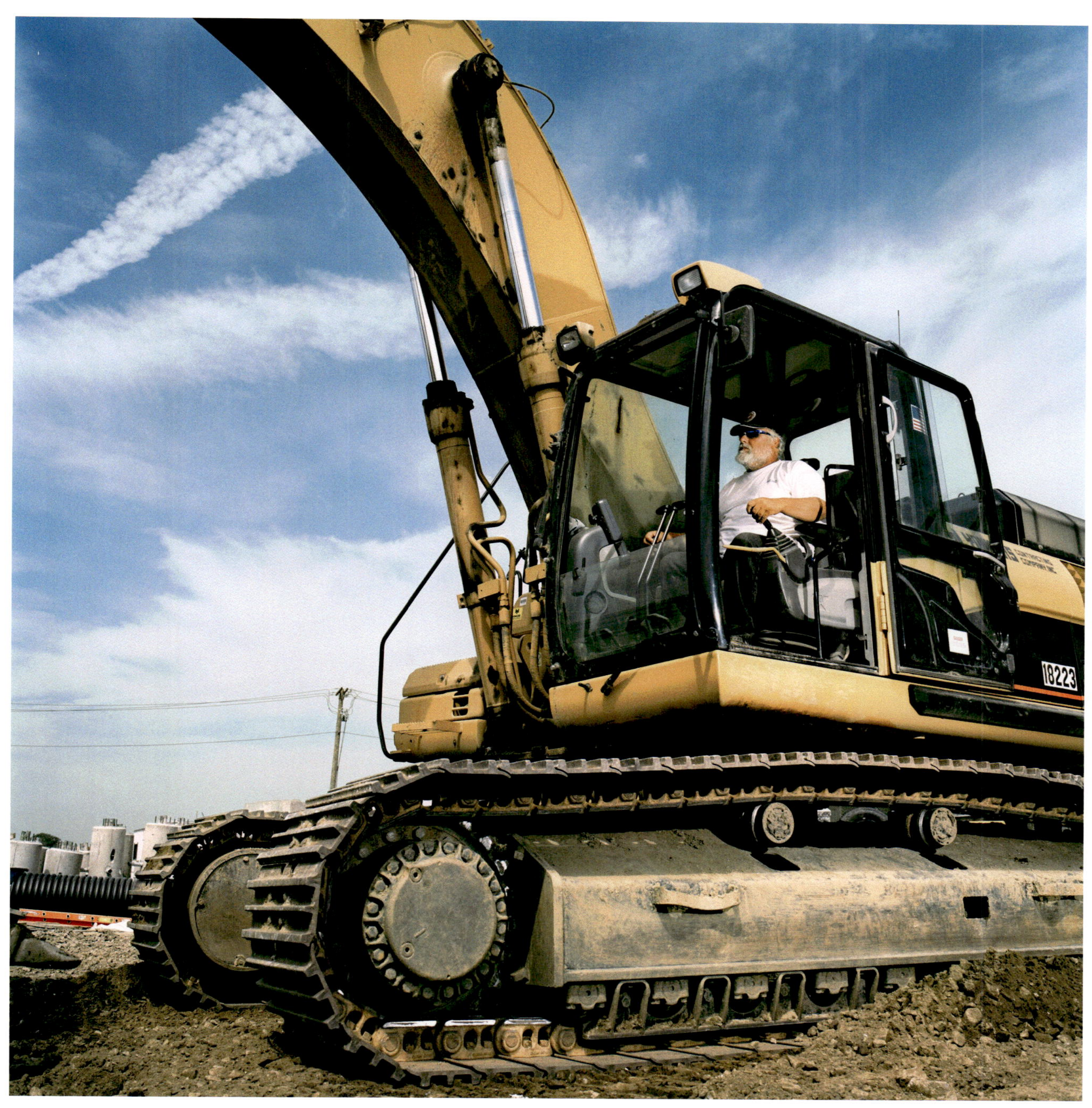

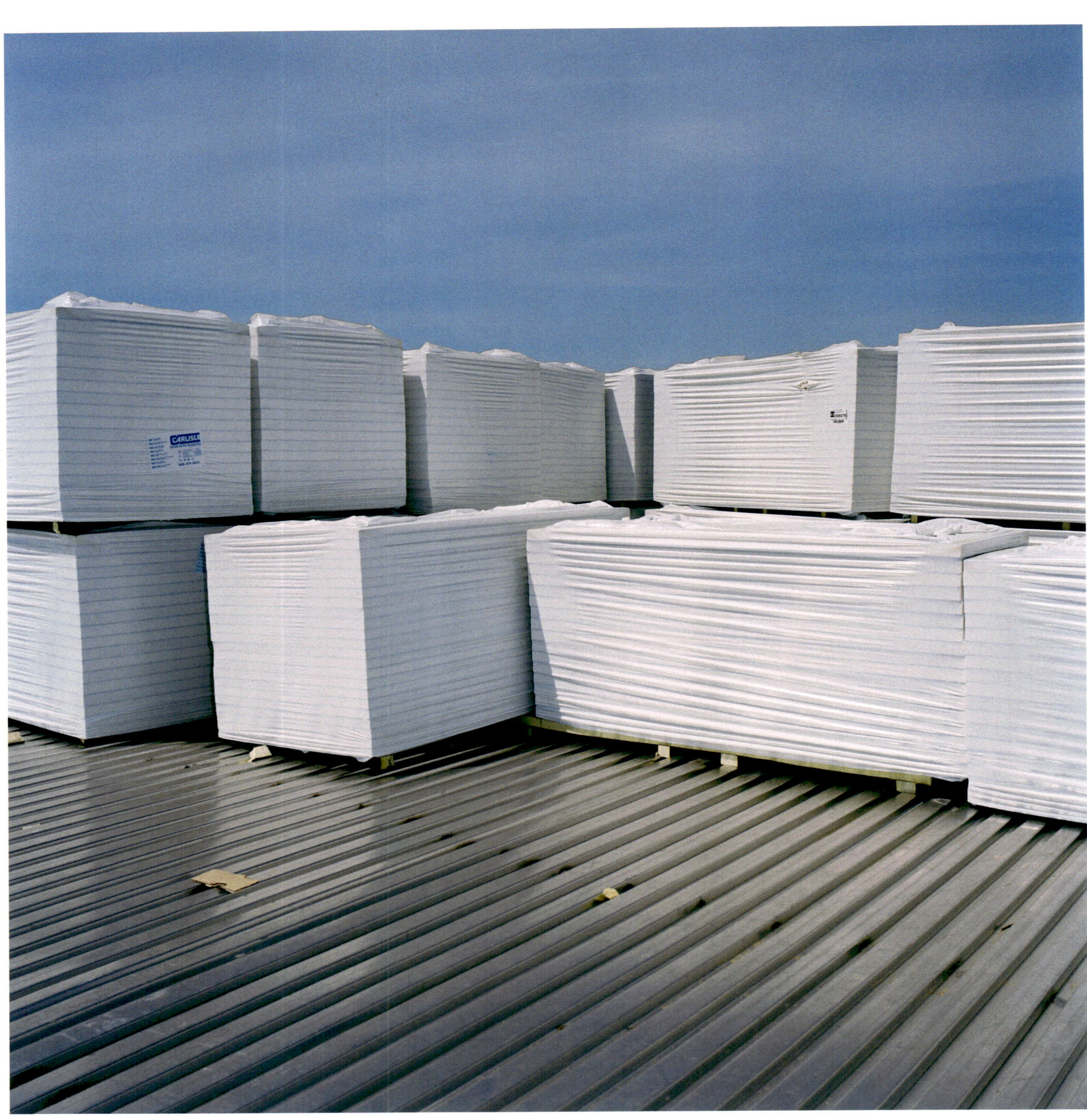

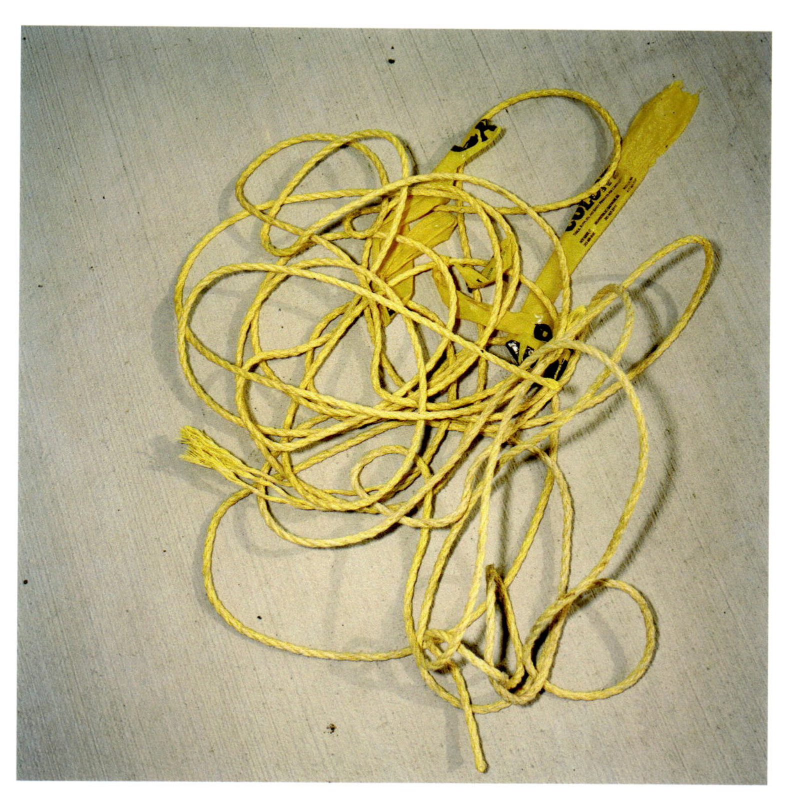
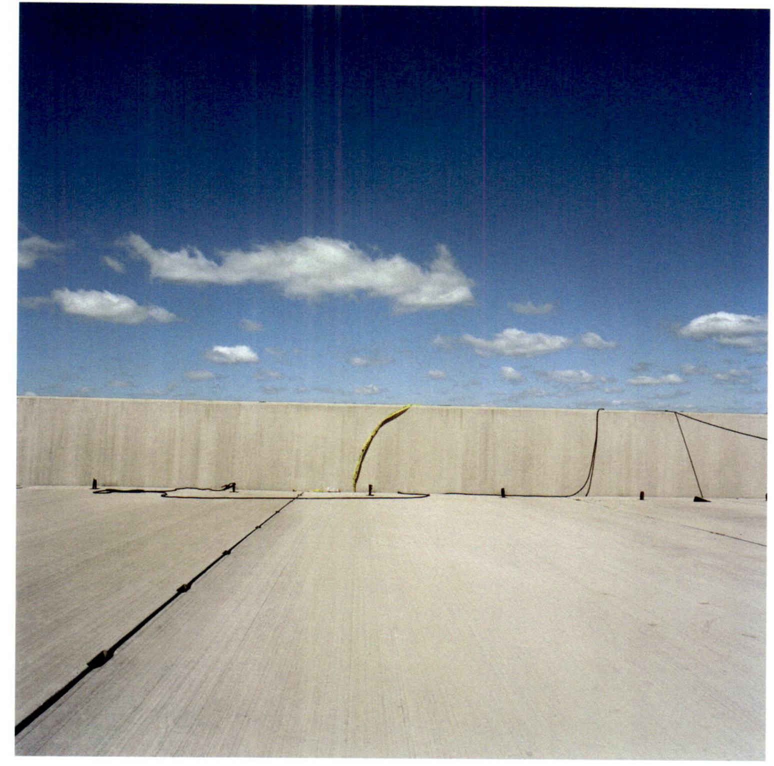

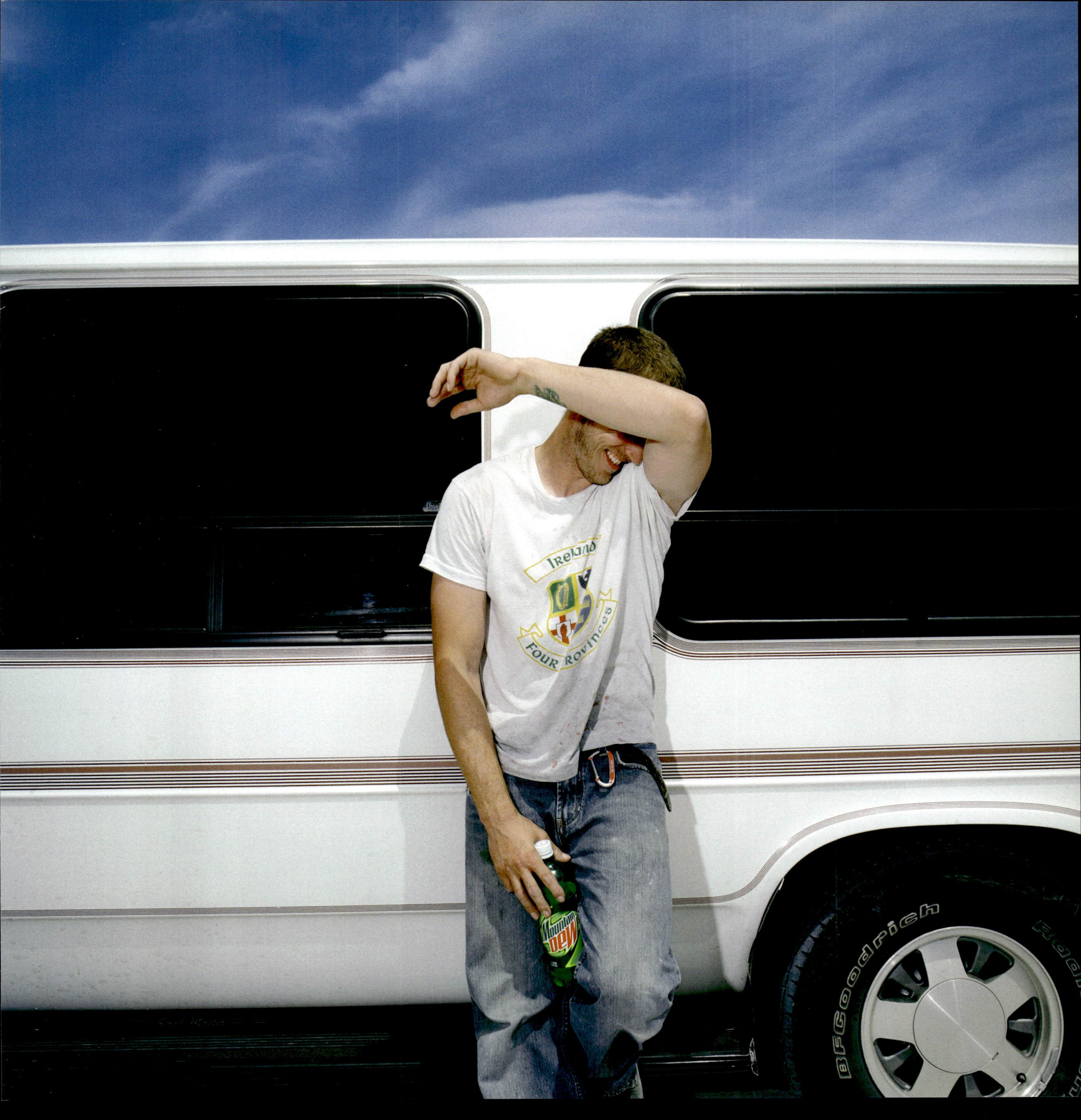

Ireland
FOUR Rovinces
Mountain Dew
BFGoodrich

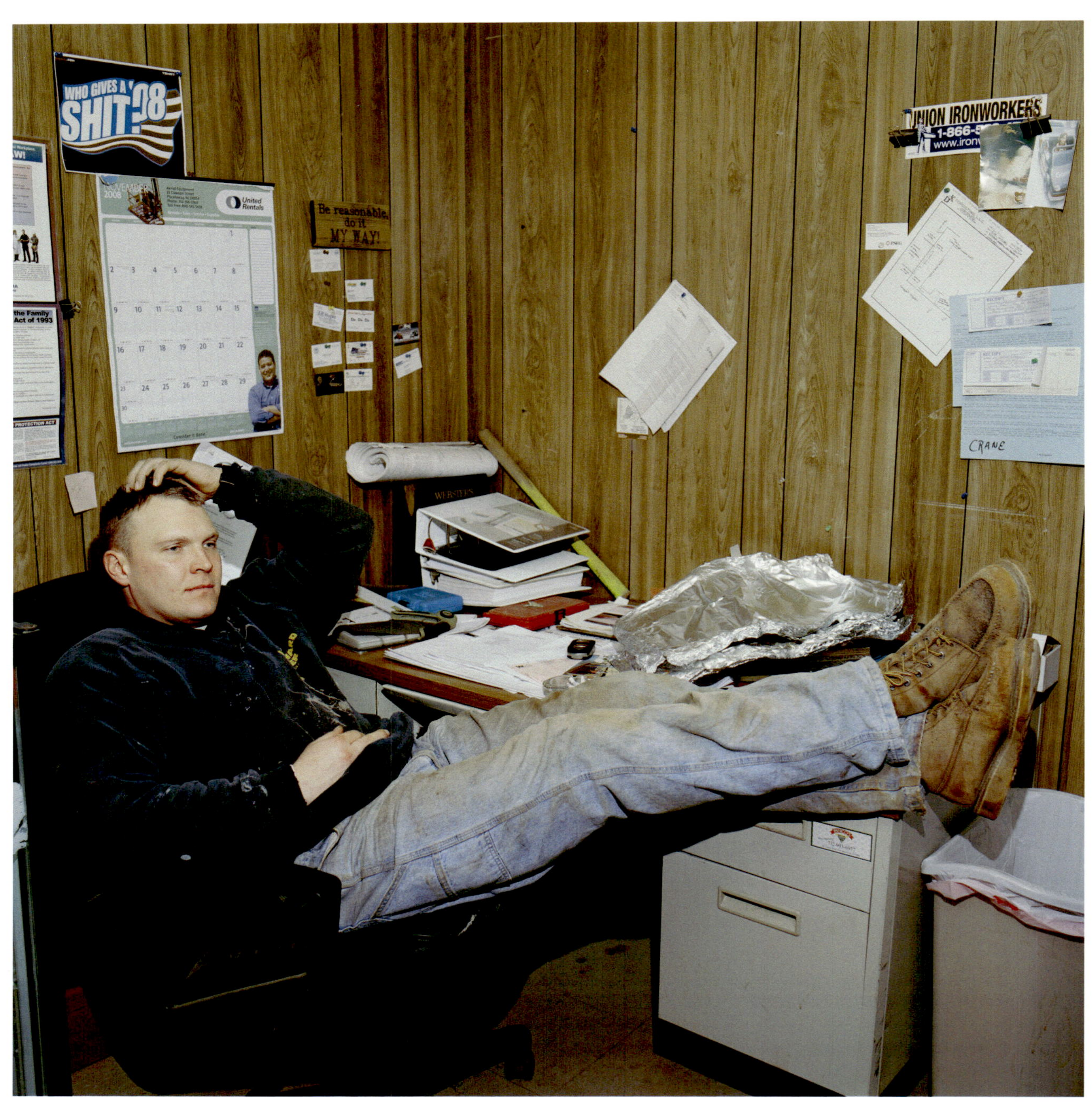

WHO GIVES A
SHIT?08
UNION IRONWORKERS
1-866-
www.ironw
Be reasonable,
do it
MY WAY!
United Rentals
NOVEMBER
2008
CRANE
the Family
Act of 1993
PROTECTION ACT

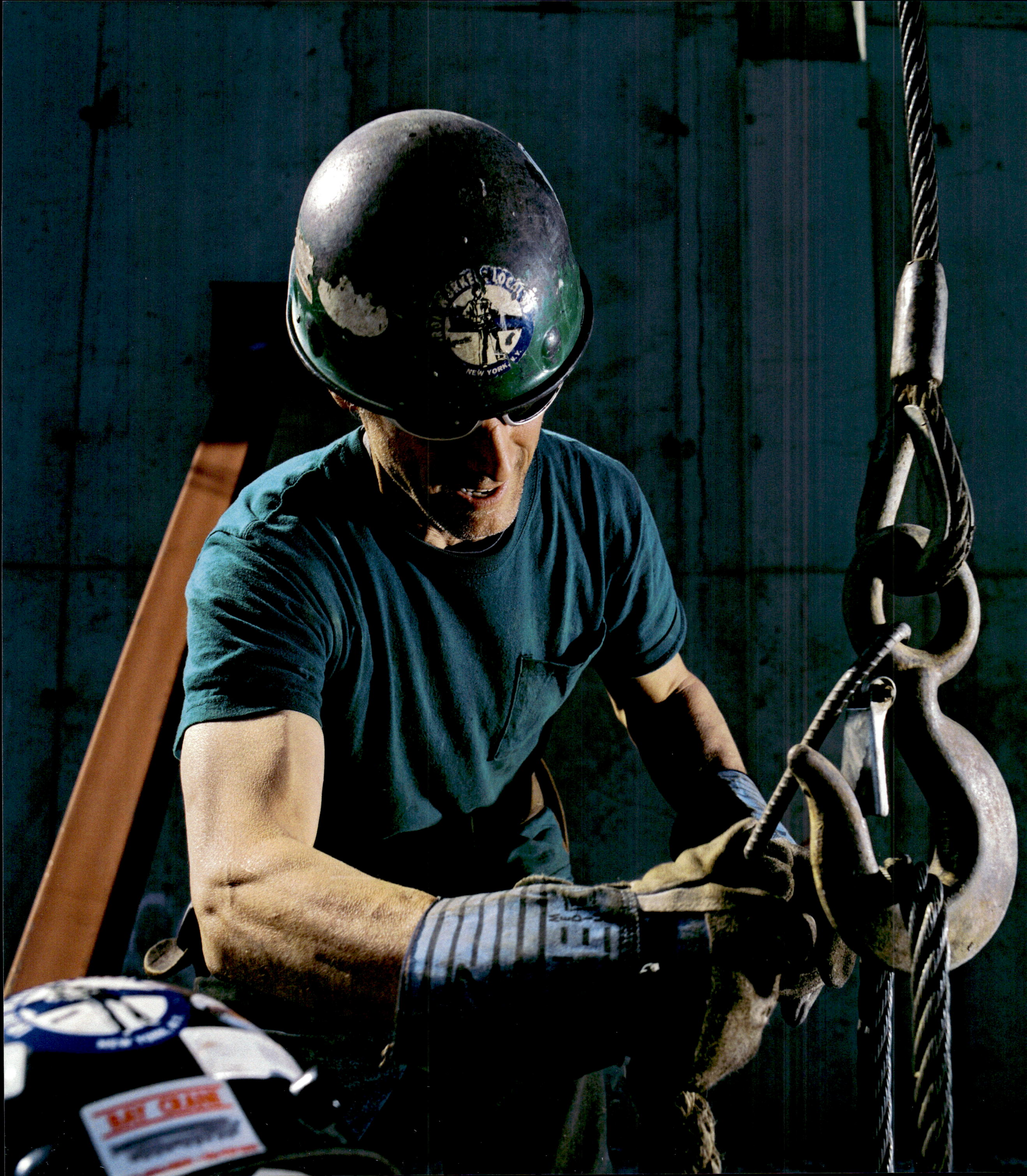

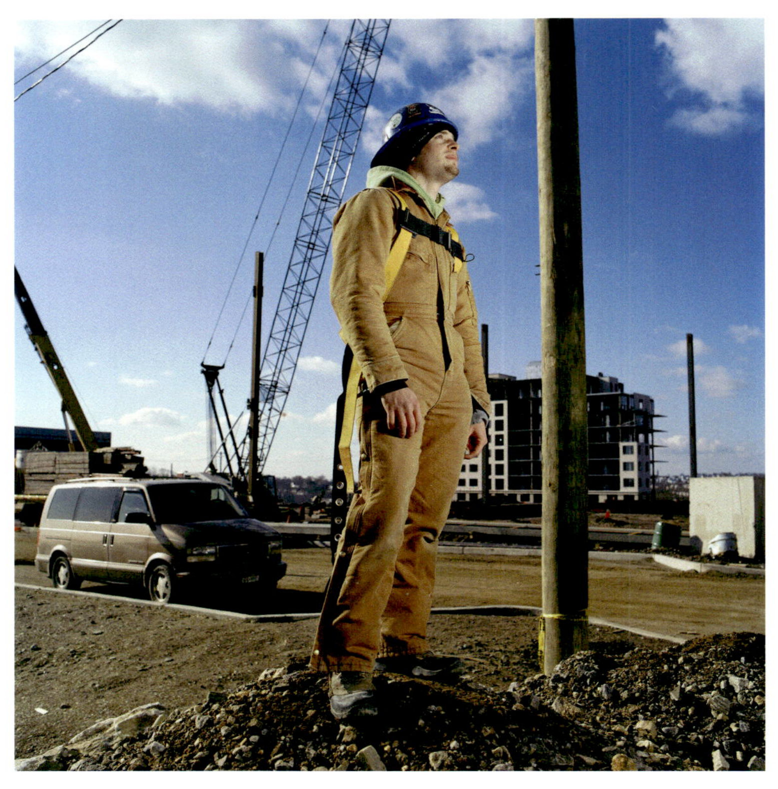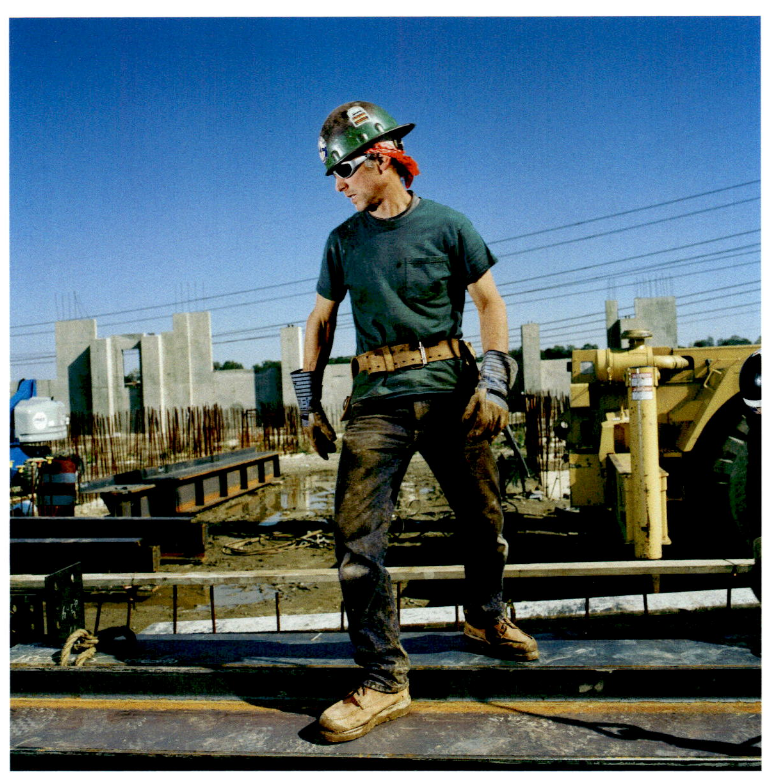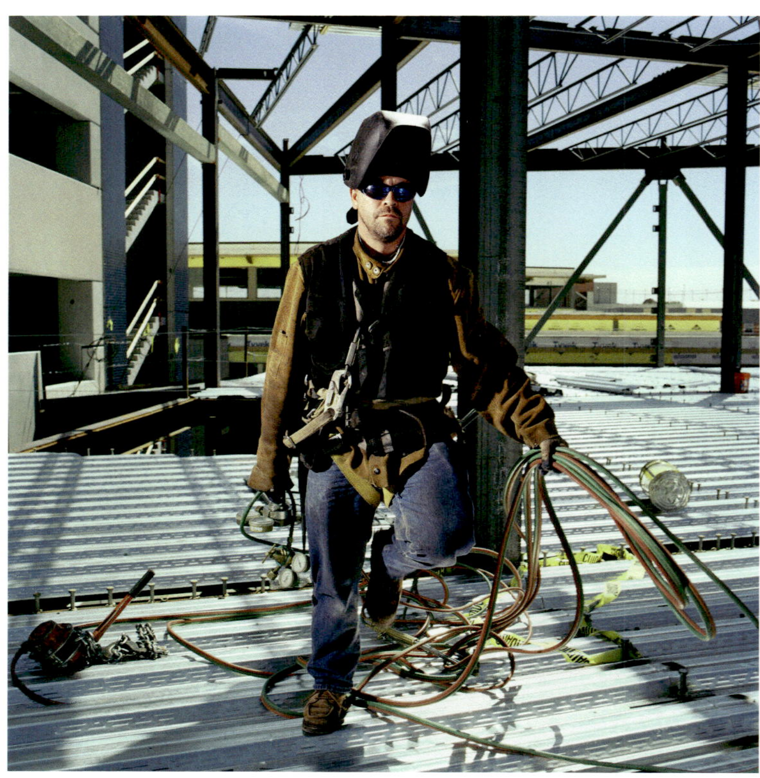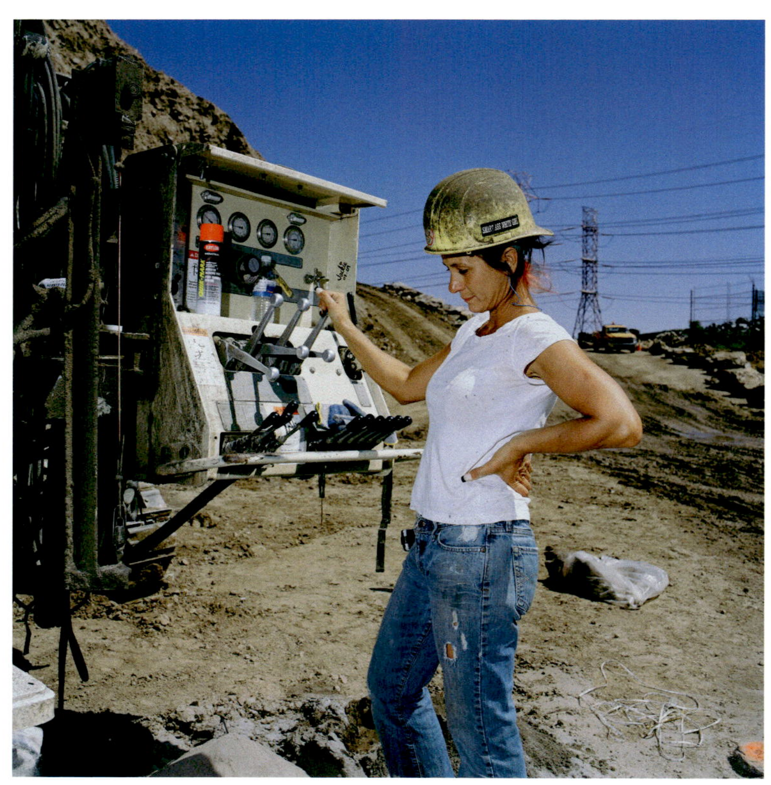

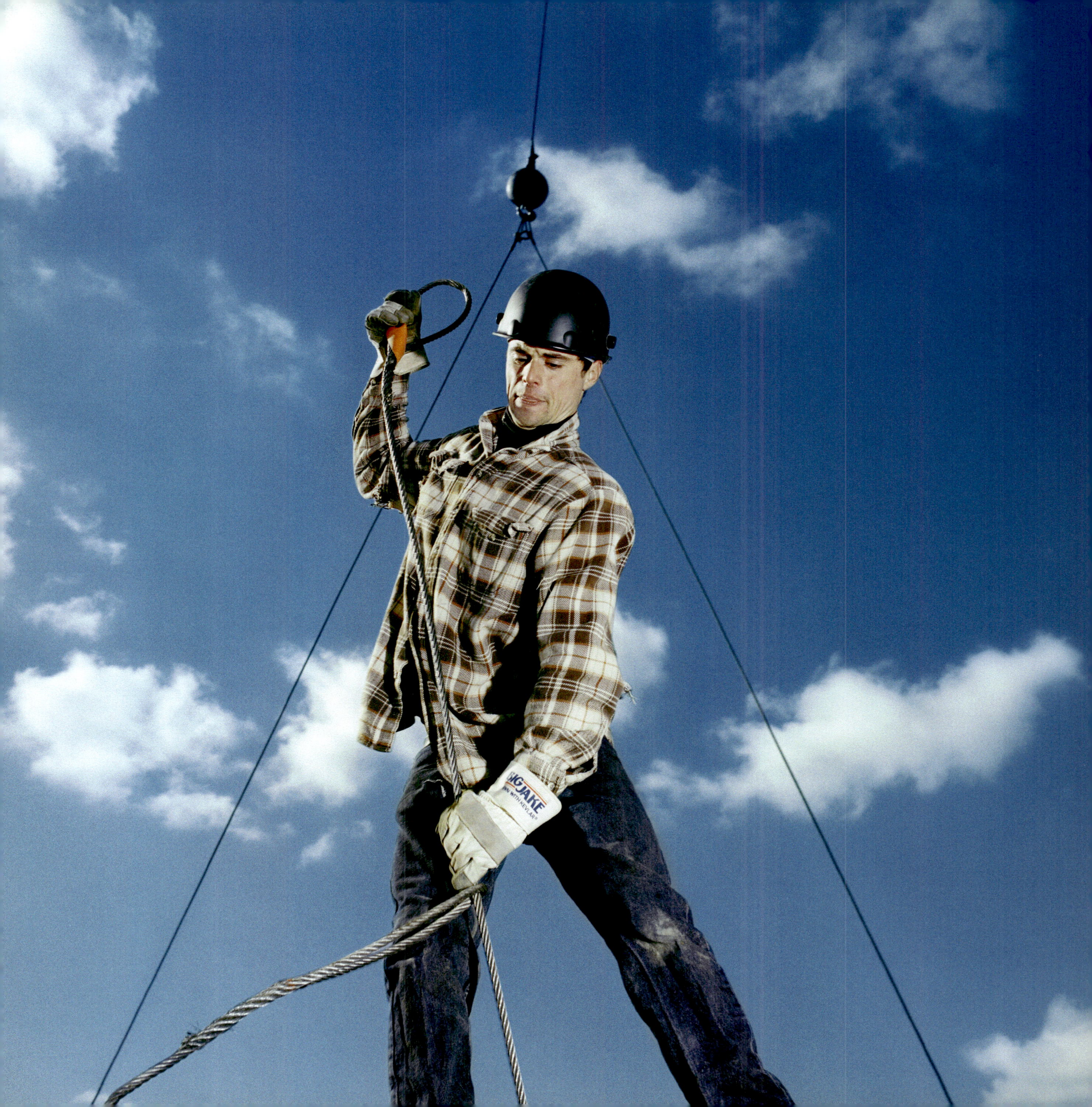

BIG JAKE
SEWN WITH KEVLAR®

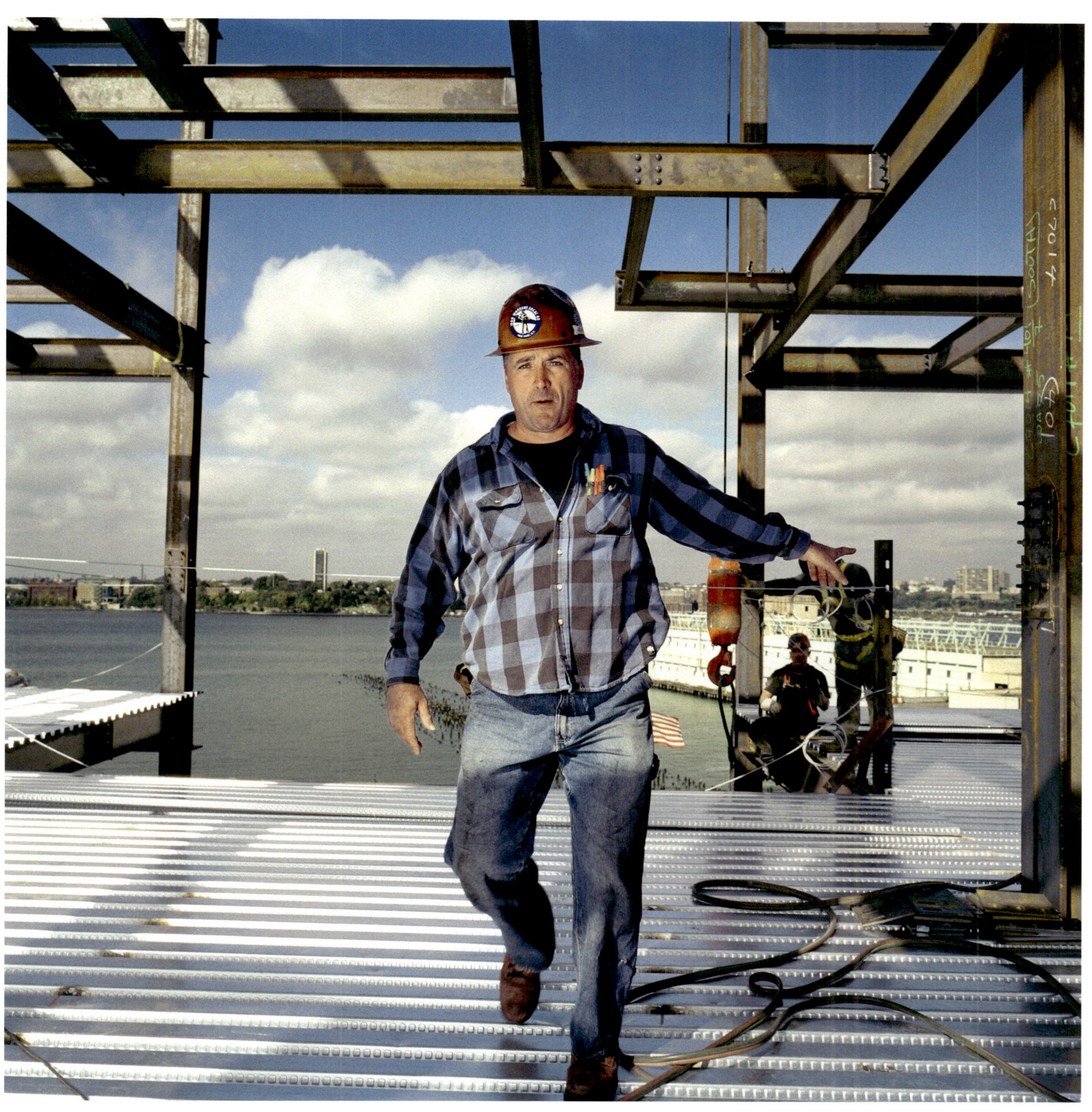

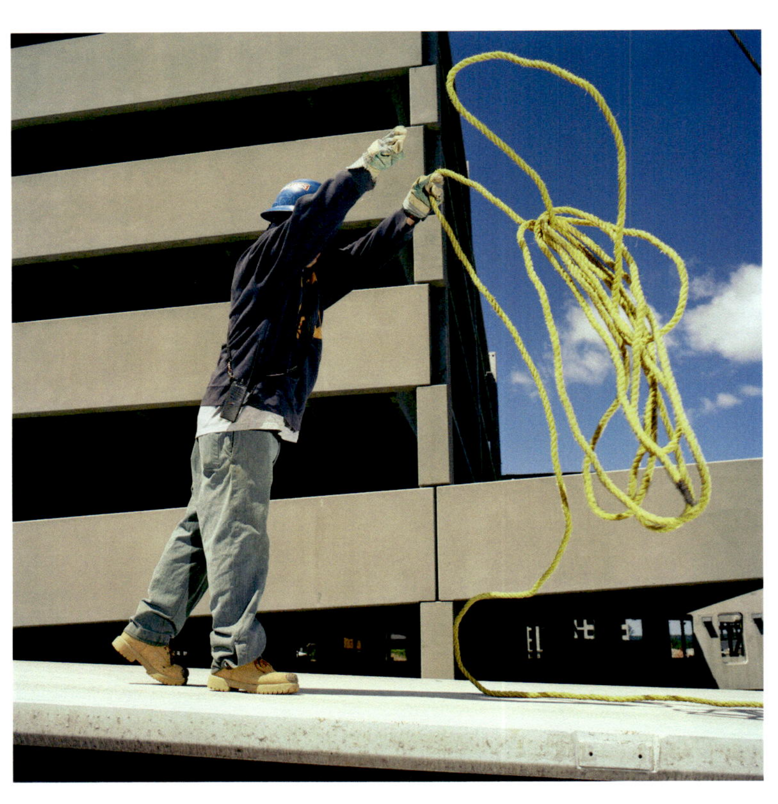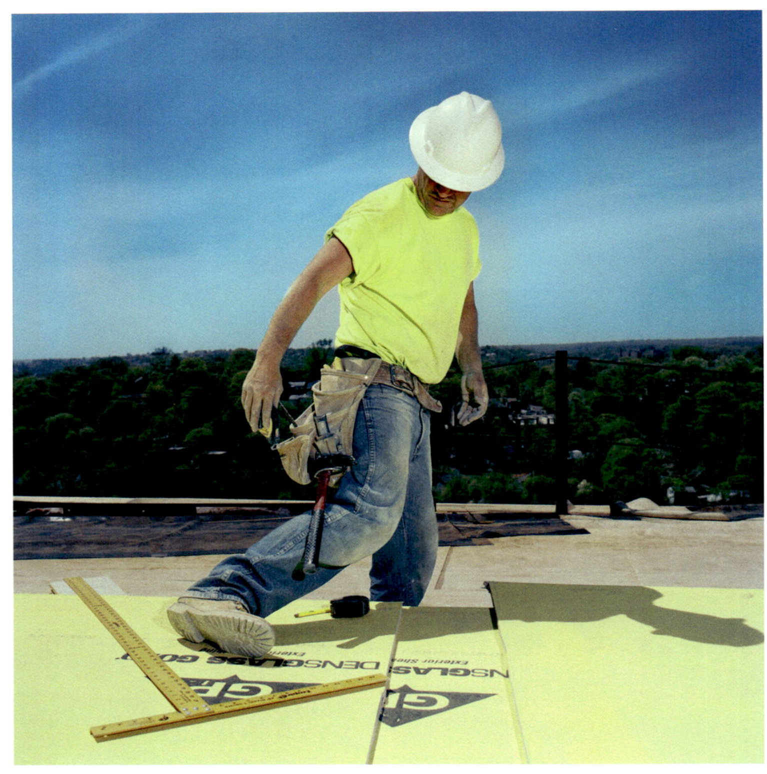

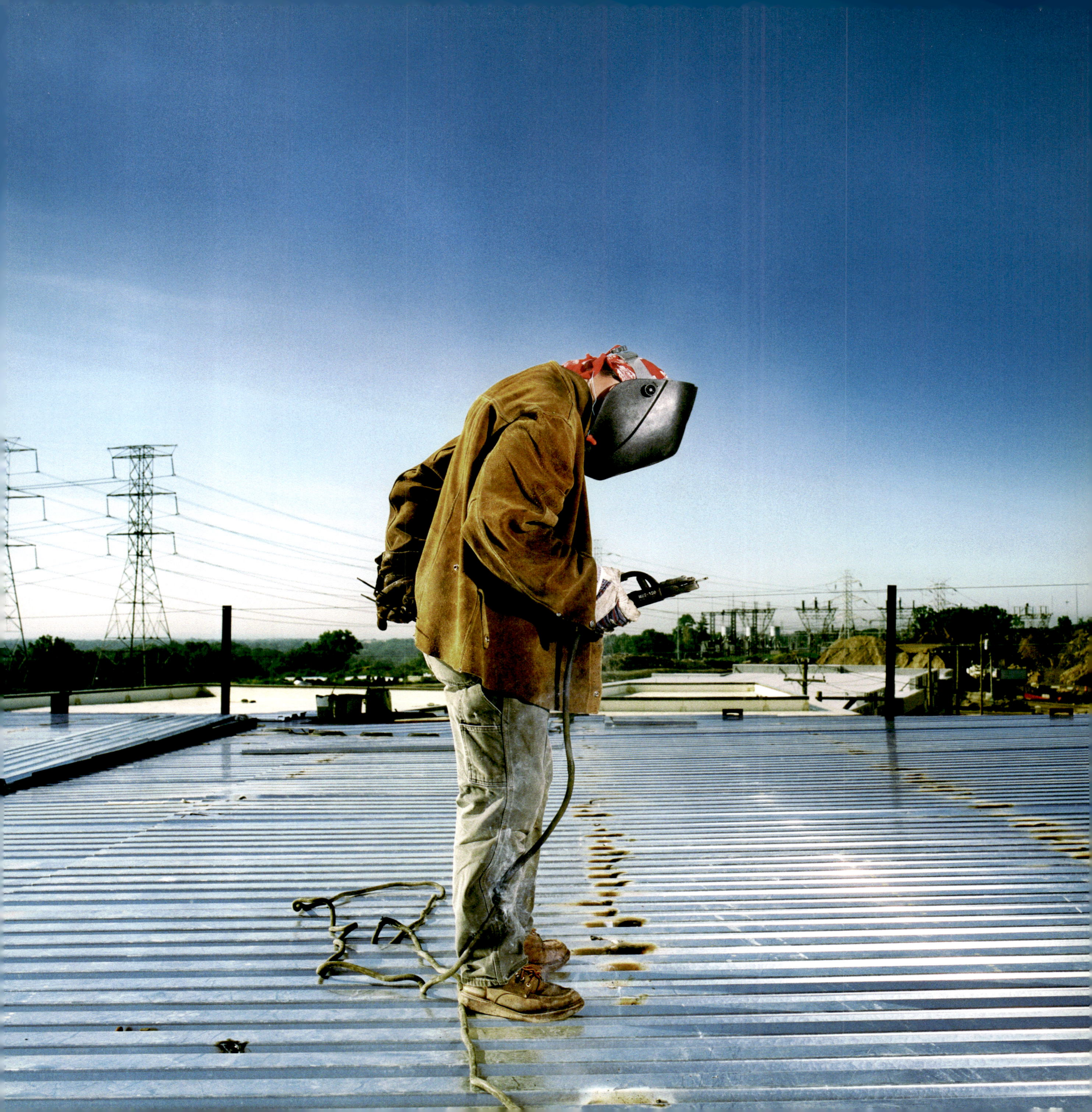

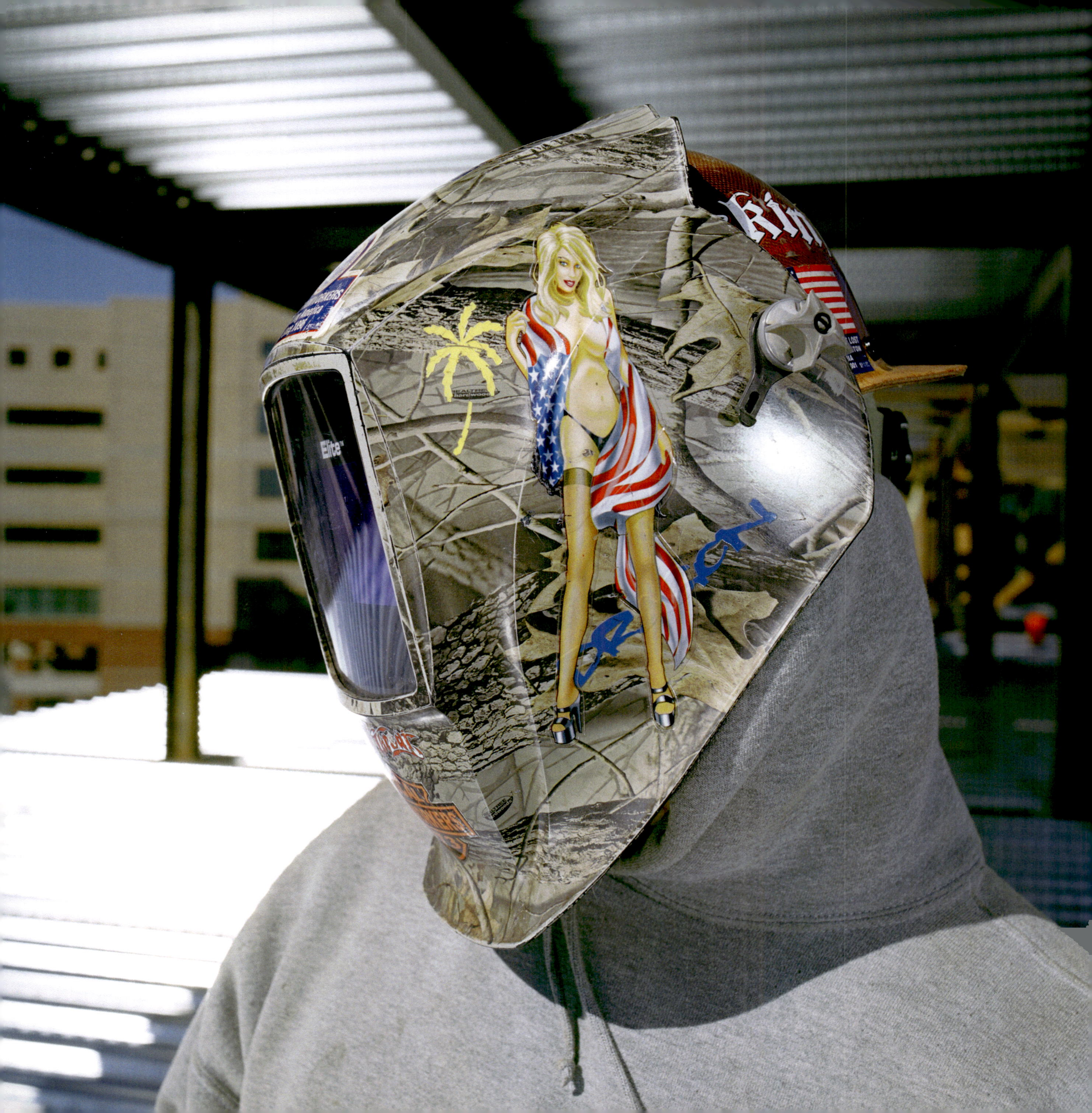

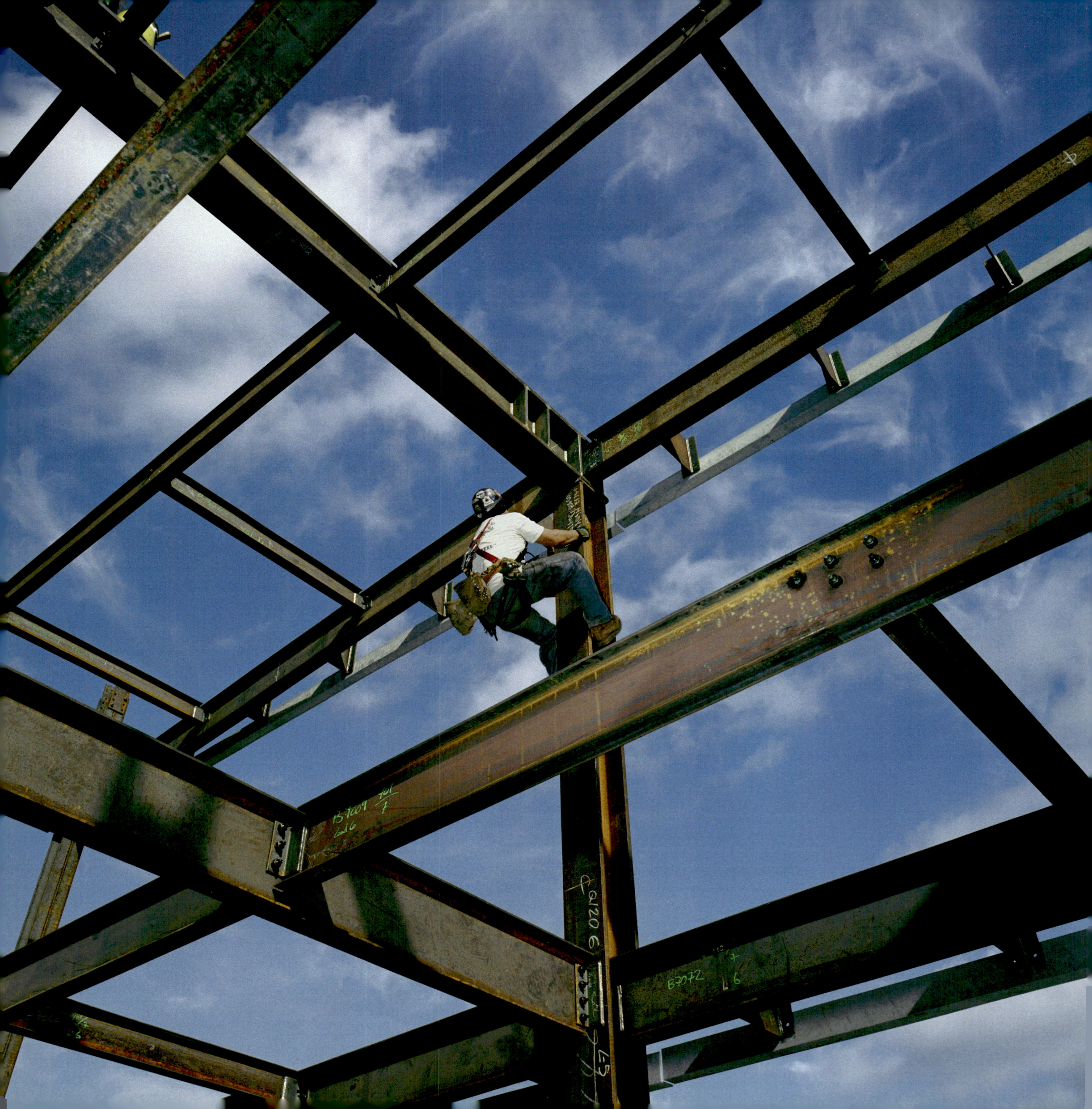

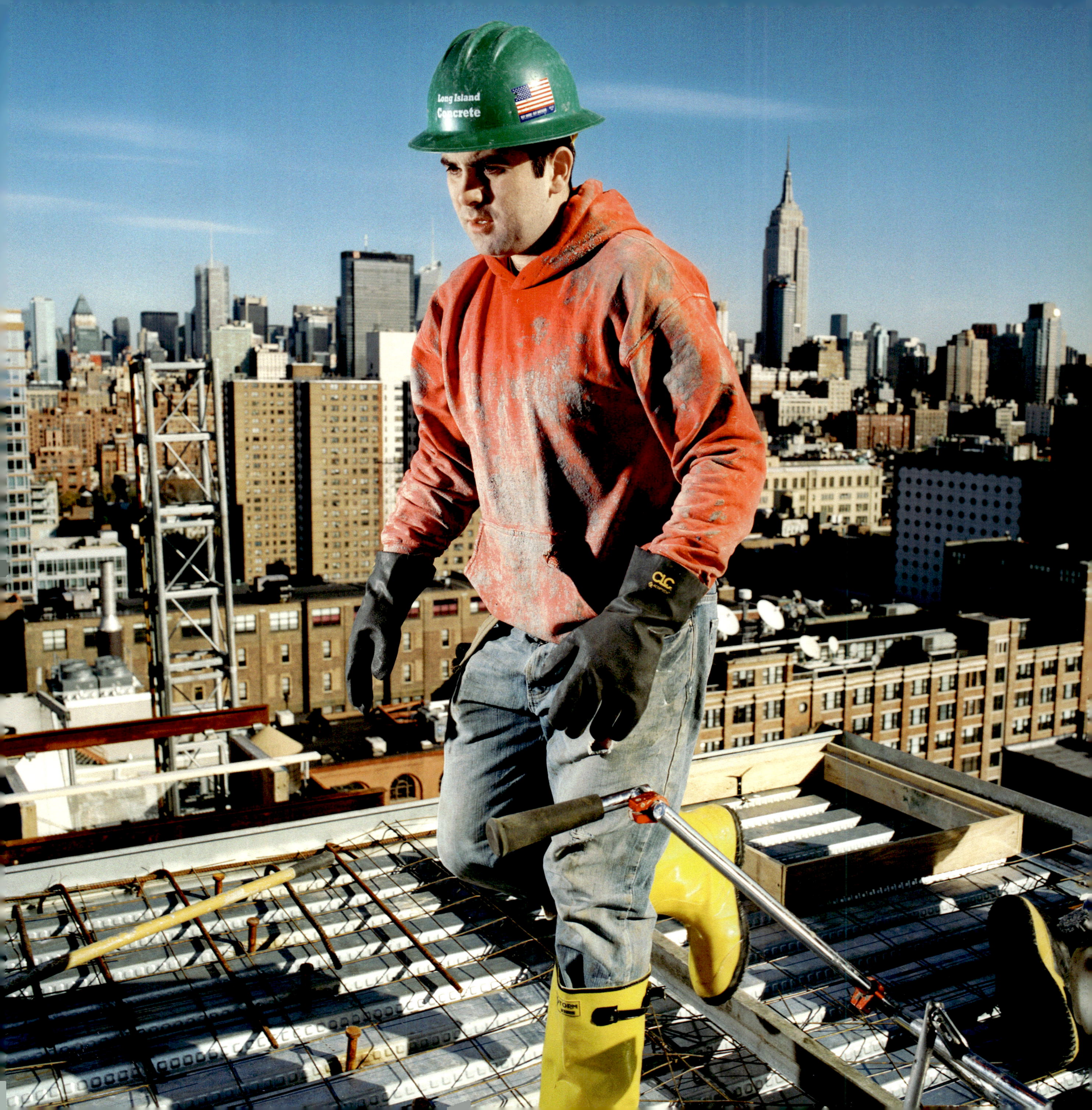
Long Island
Concrete

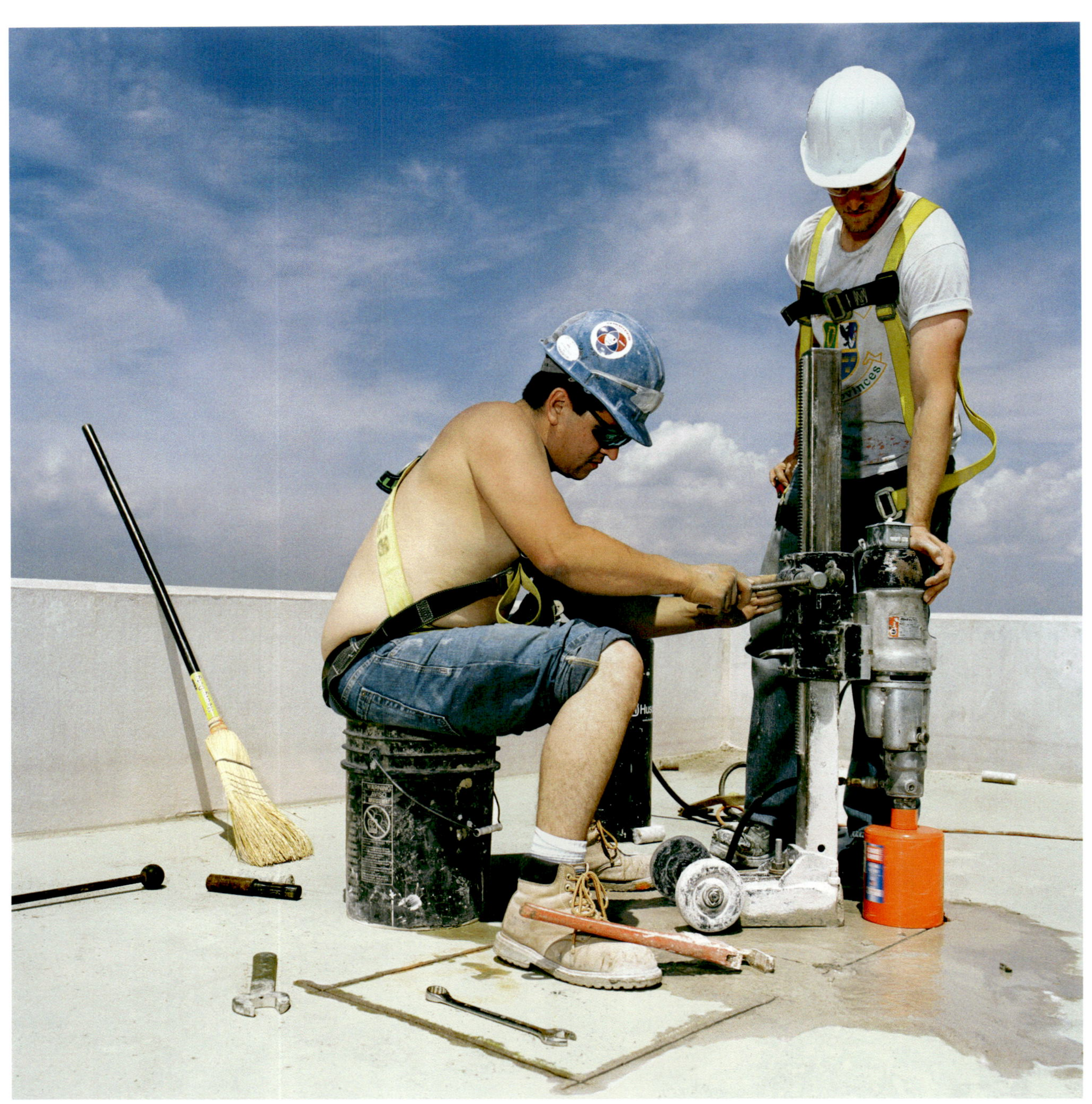

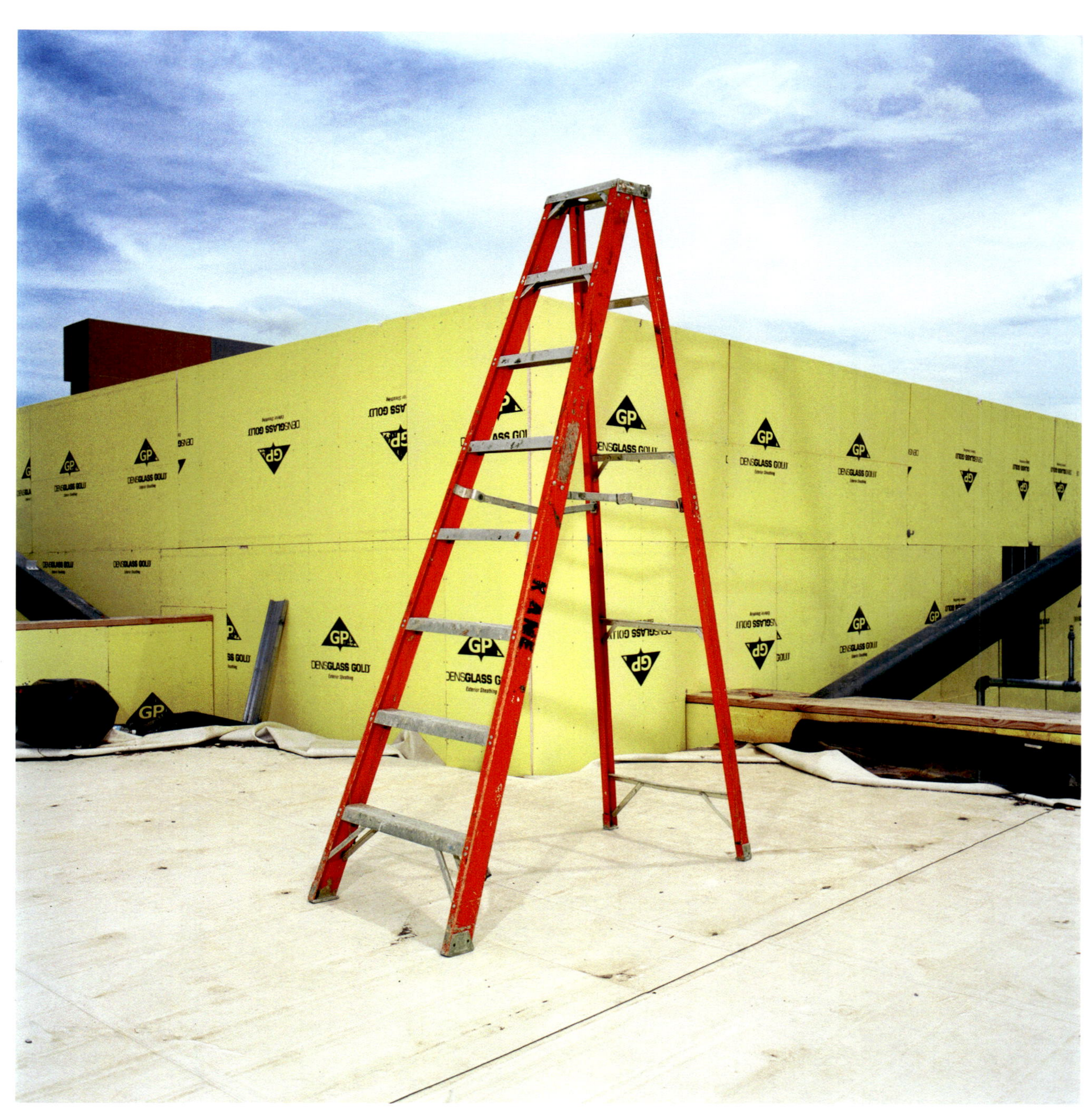

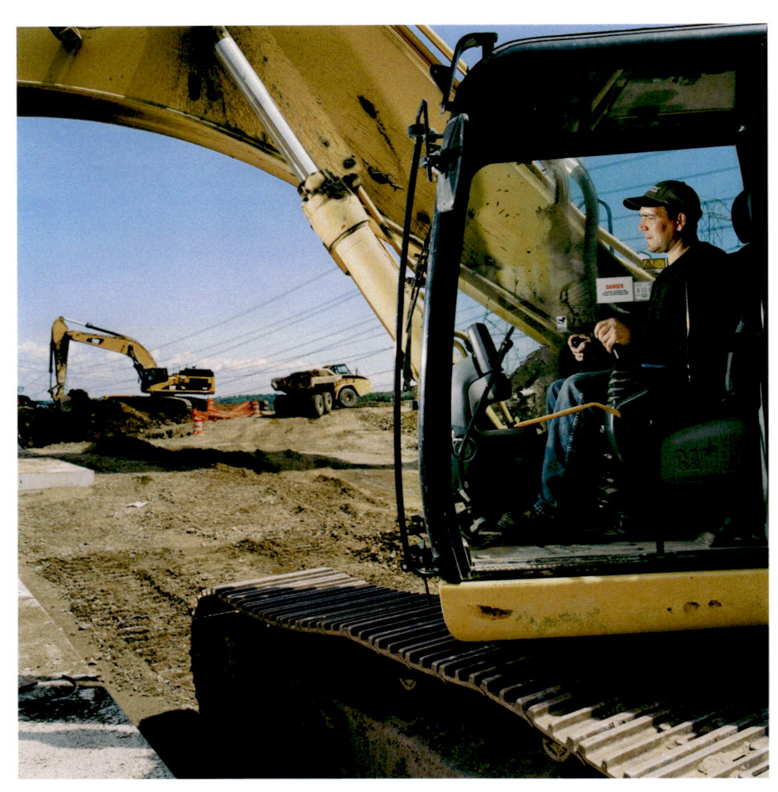

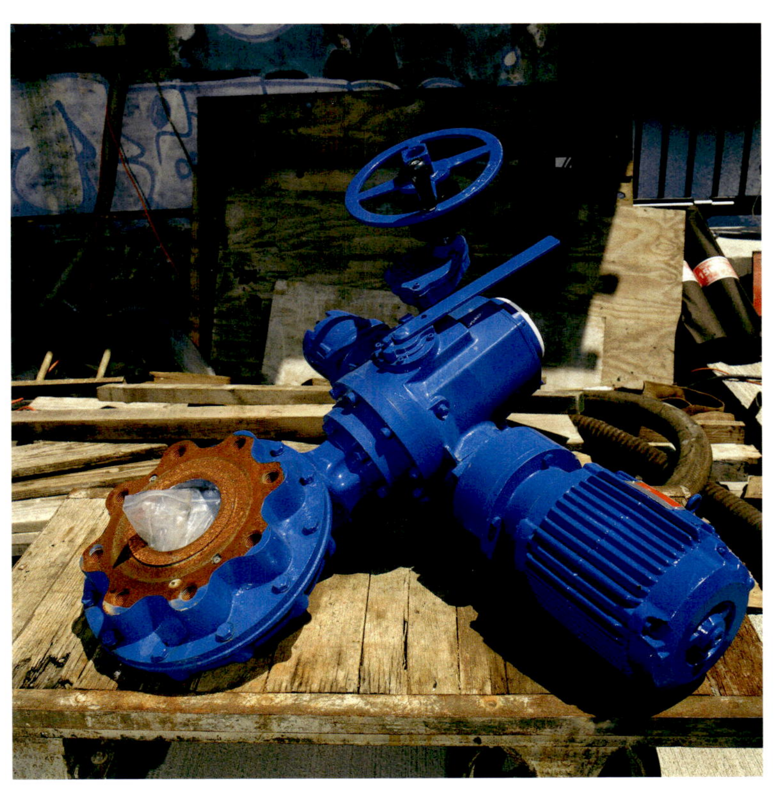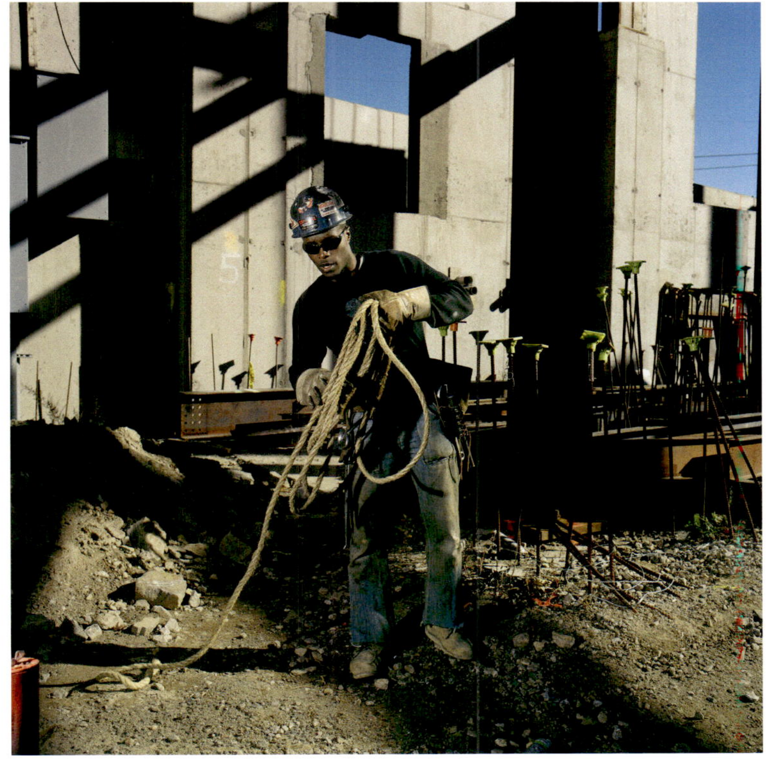

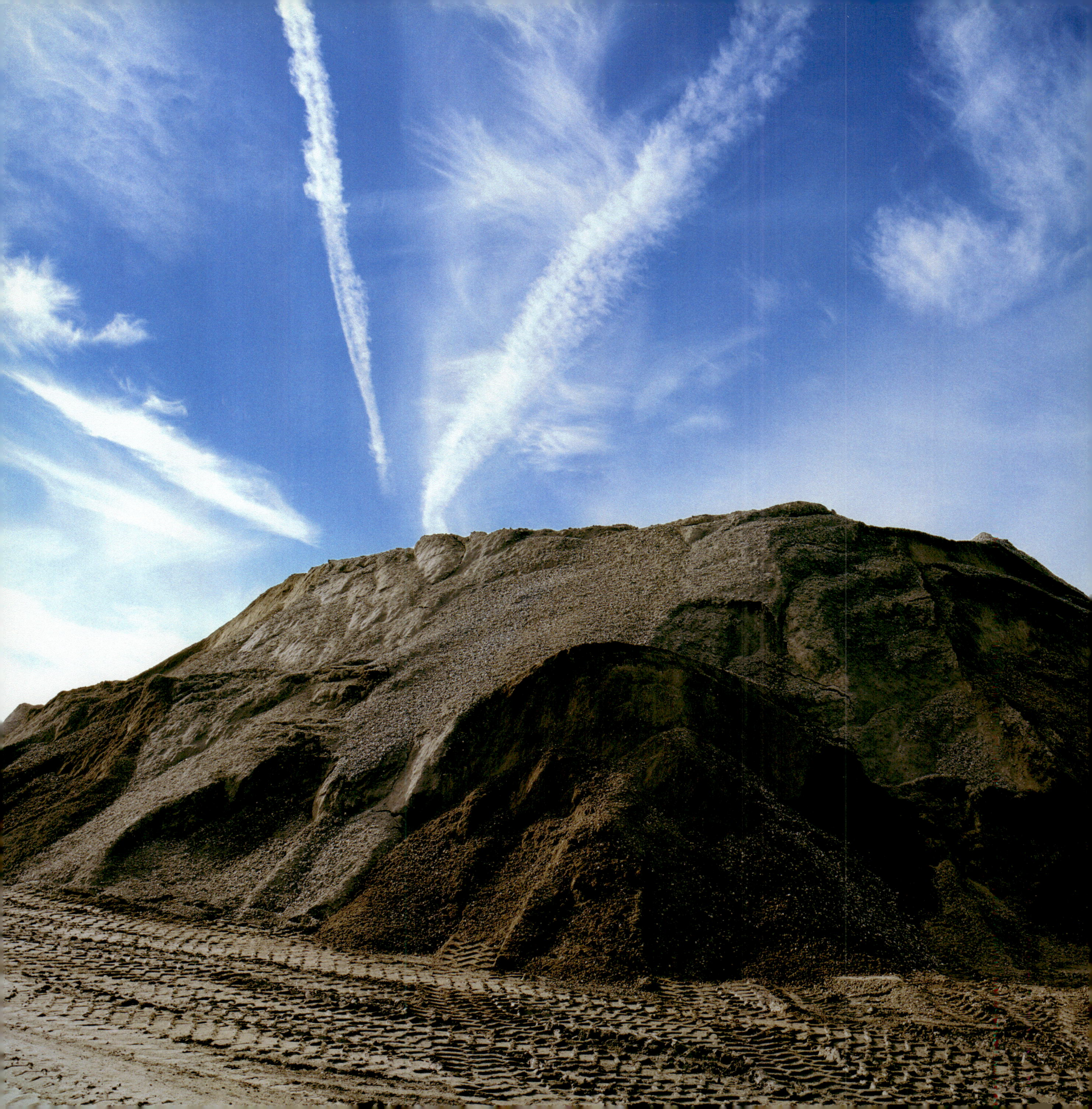

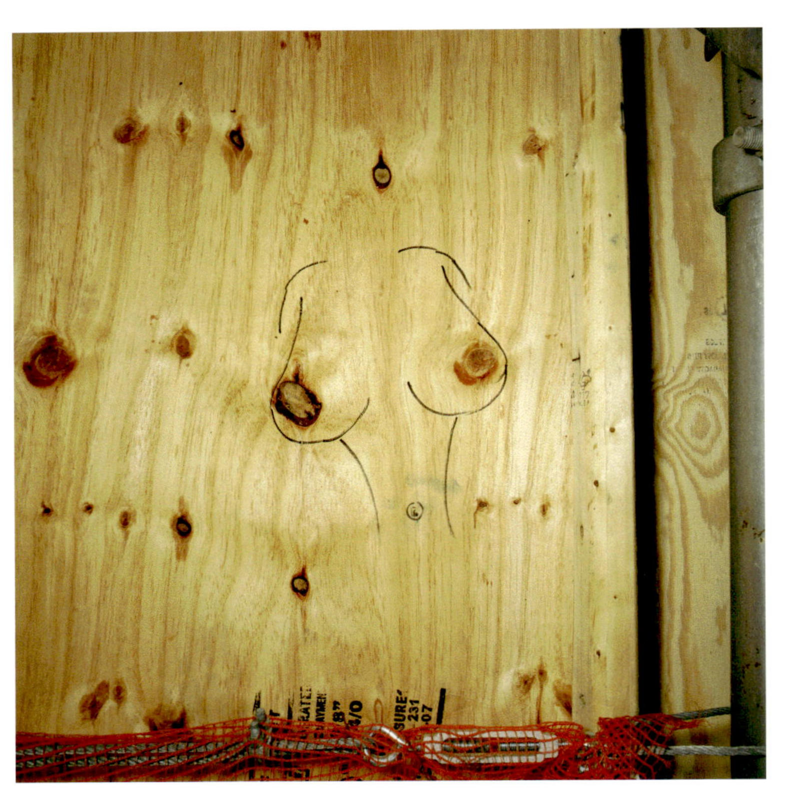
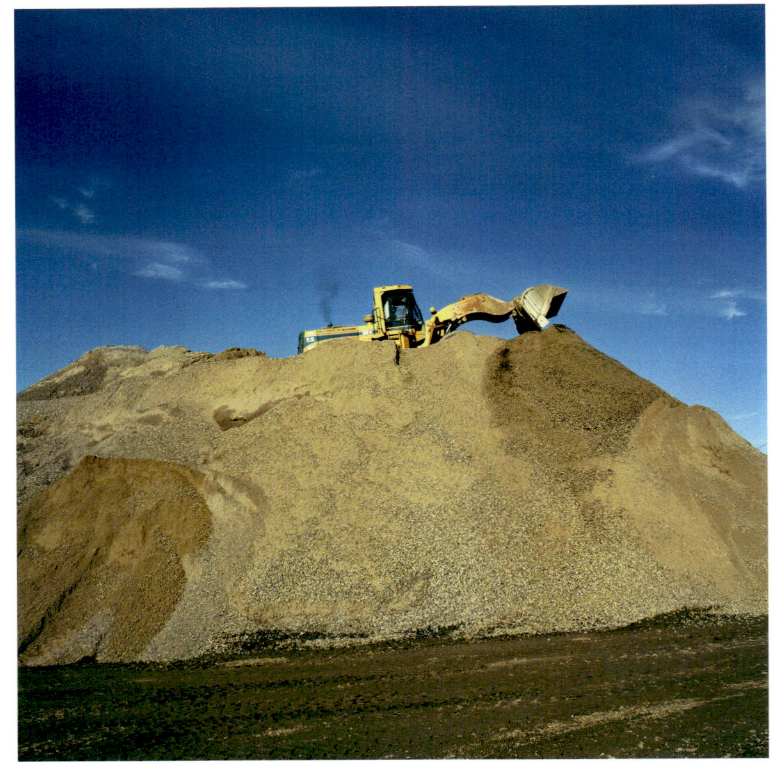

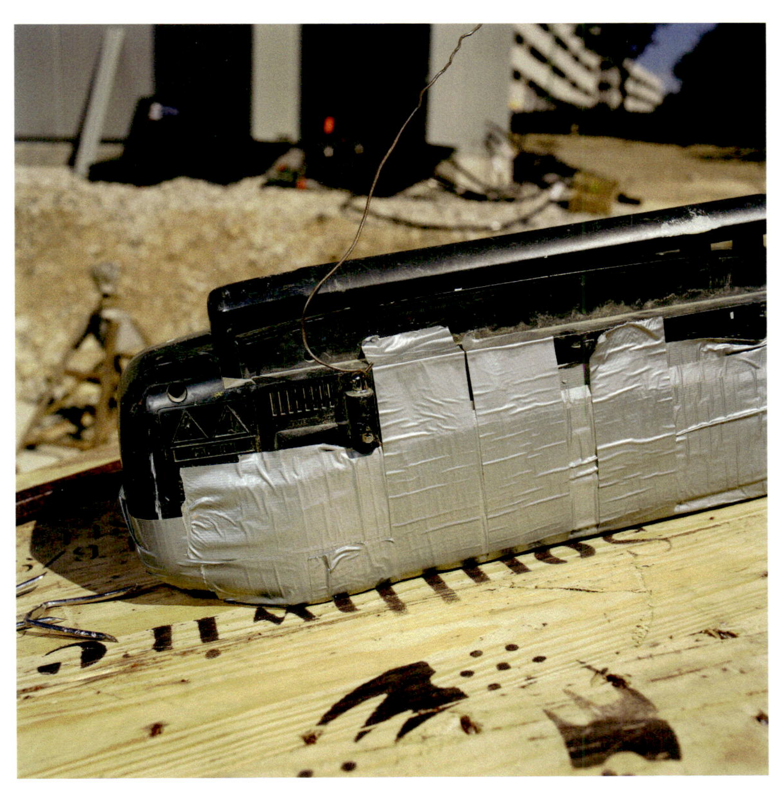 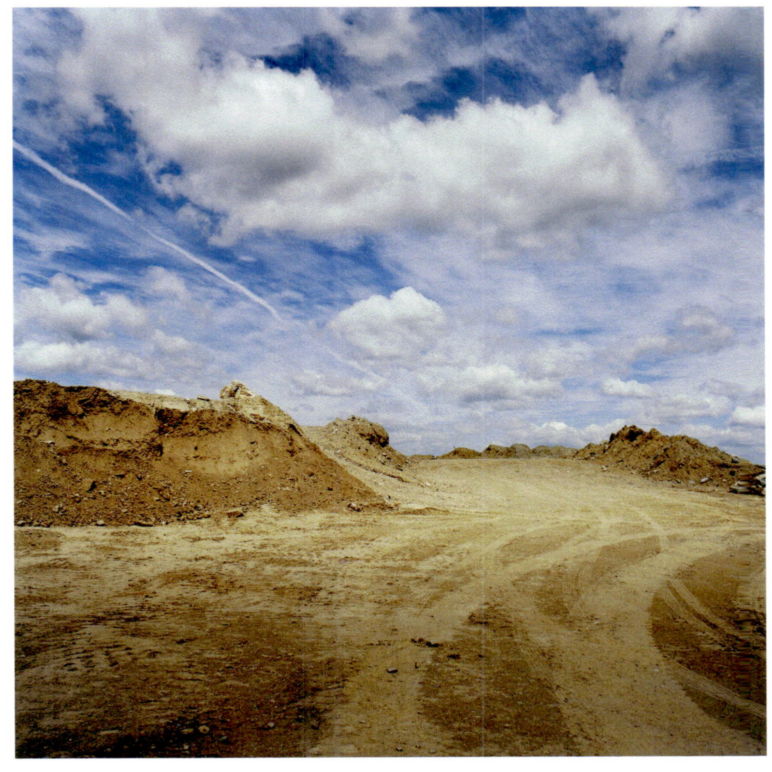

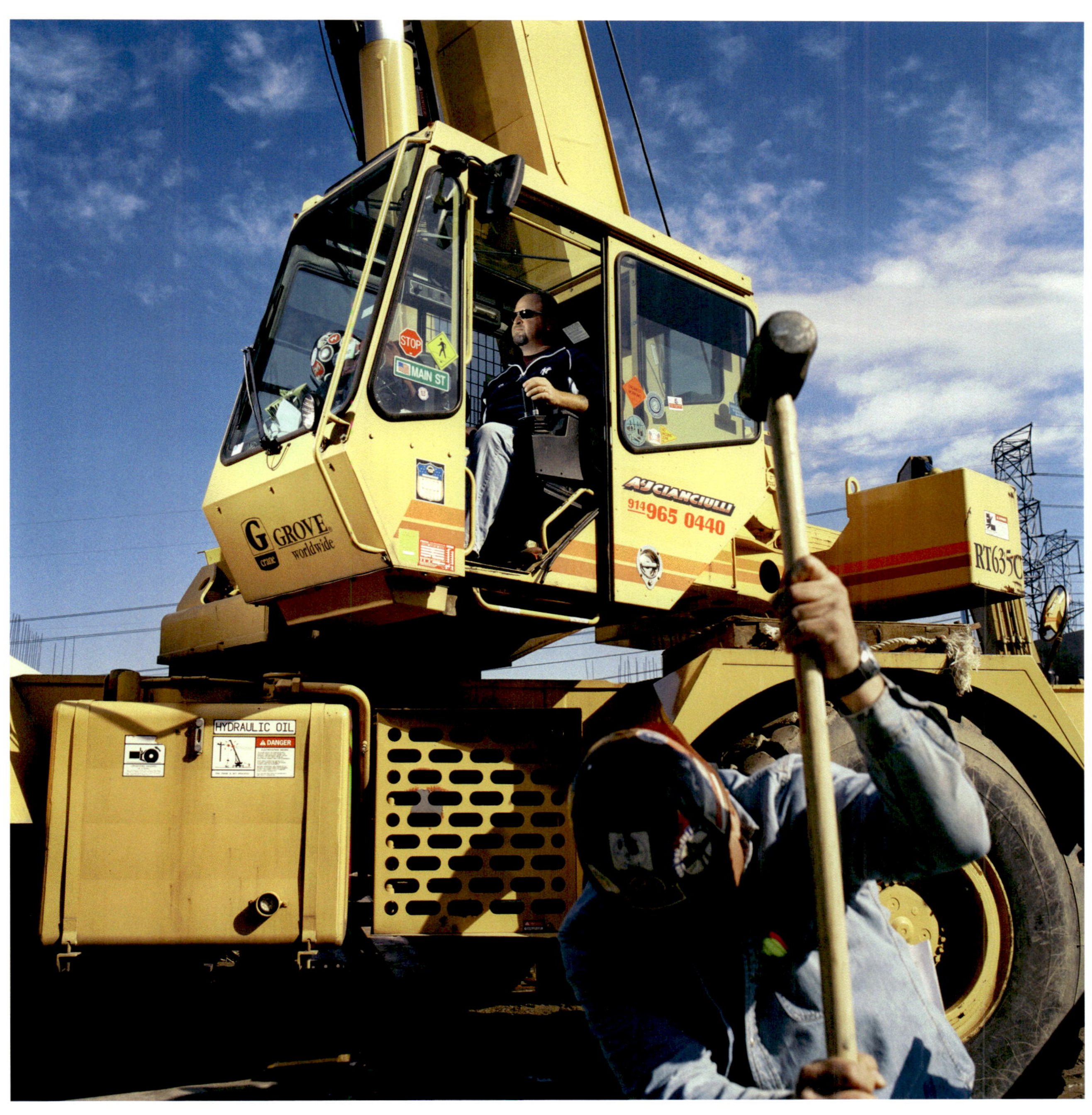

STOP
MAIN ST
G GROVE
worldwide
A J CIANCIULLI
914 965 0440
RT635C
HYDRAULIC OIL
DANGER

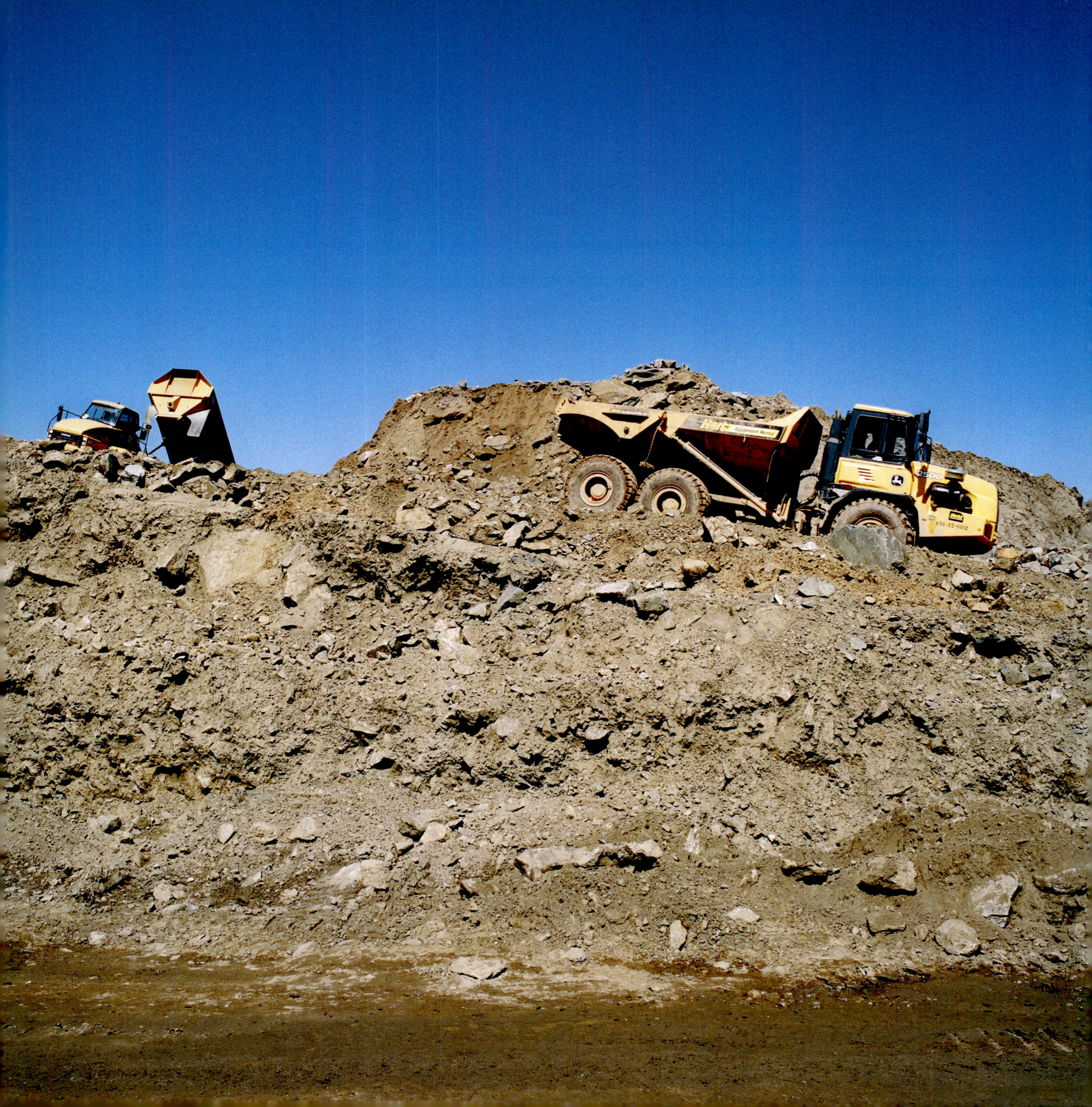

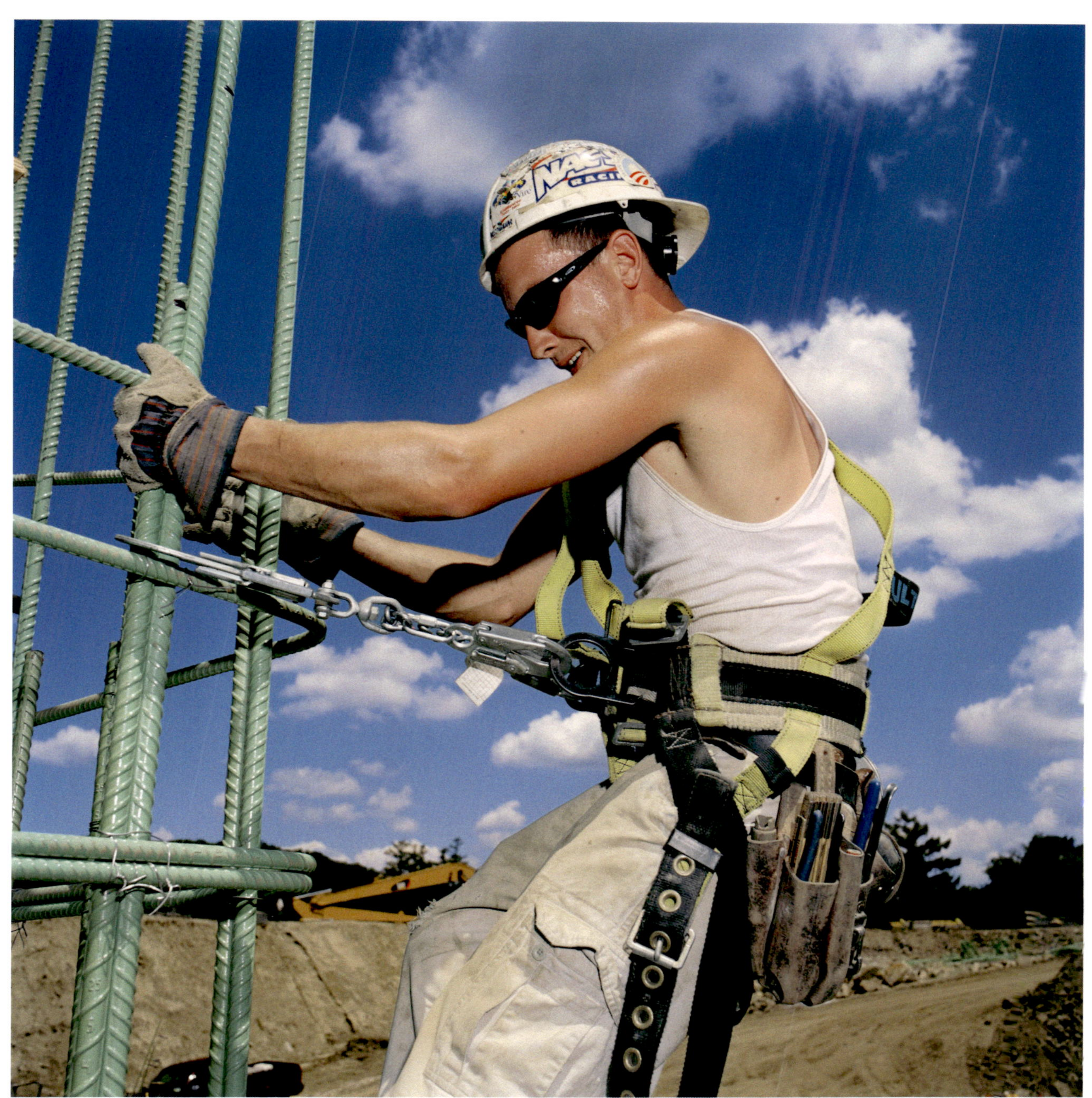

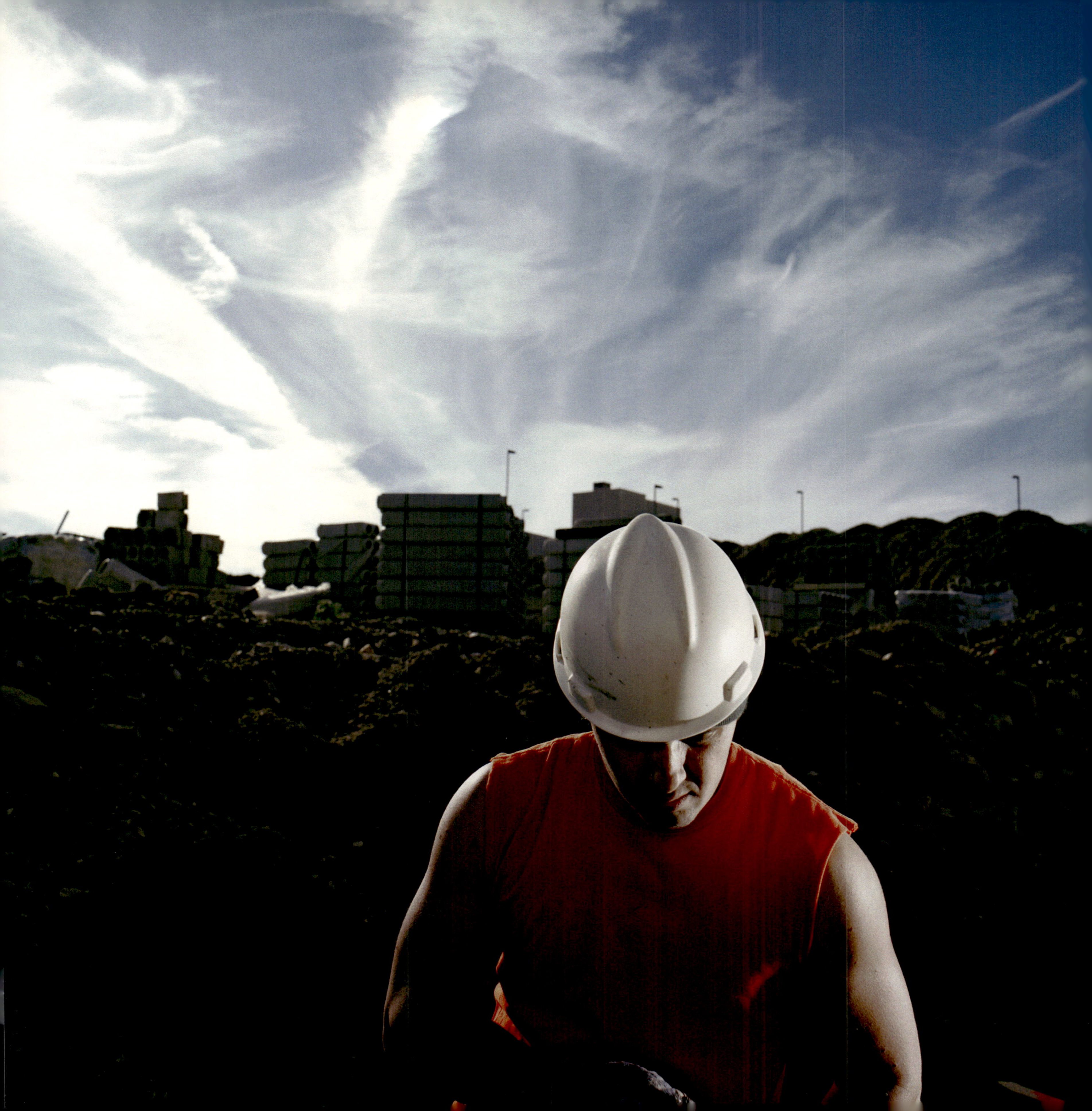

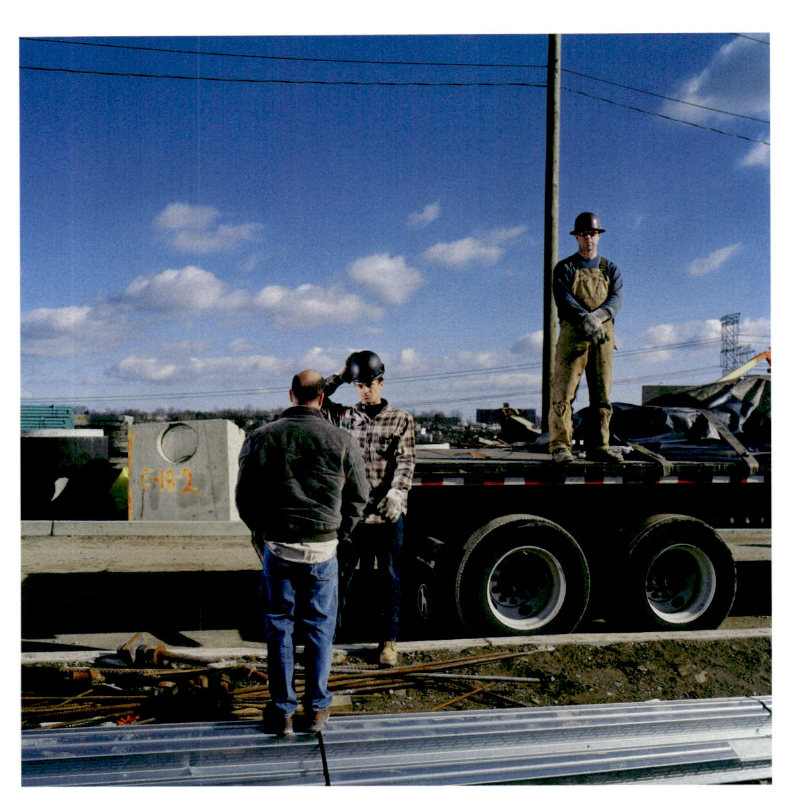

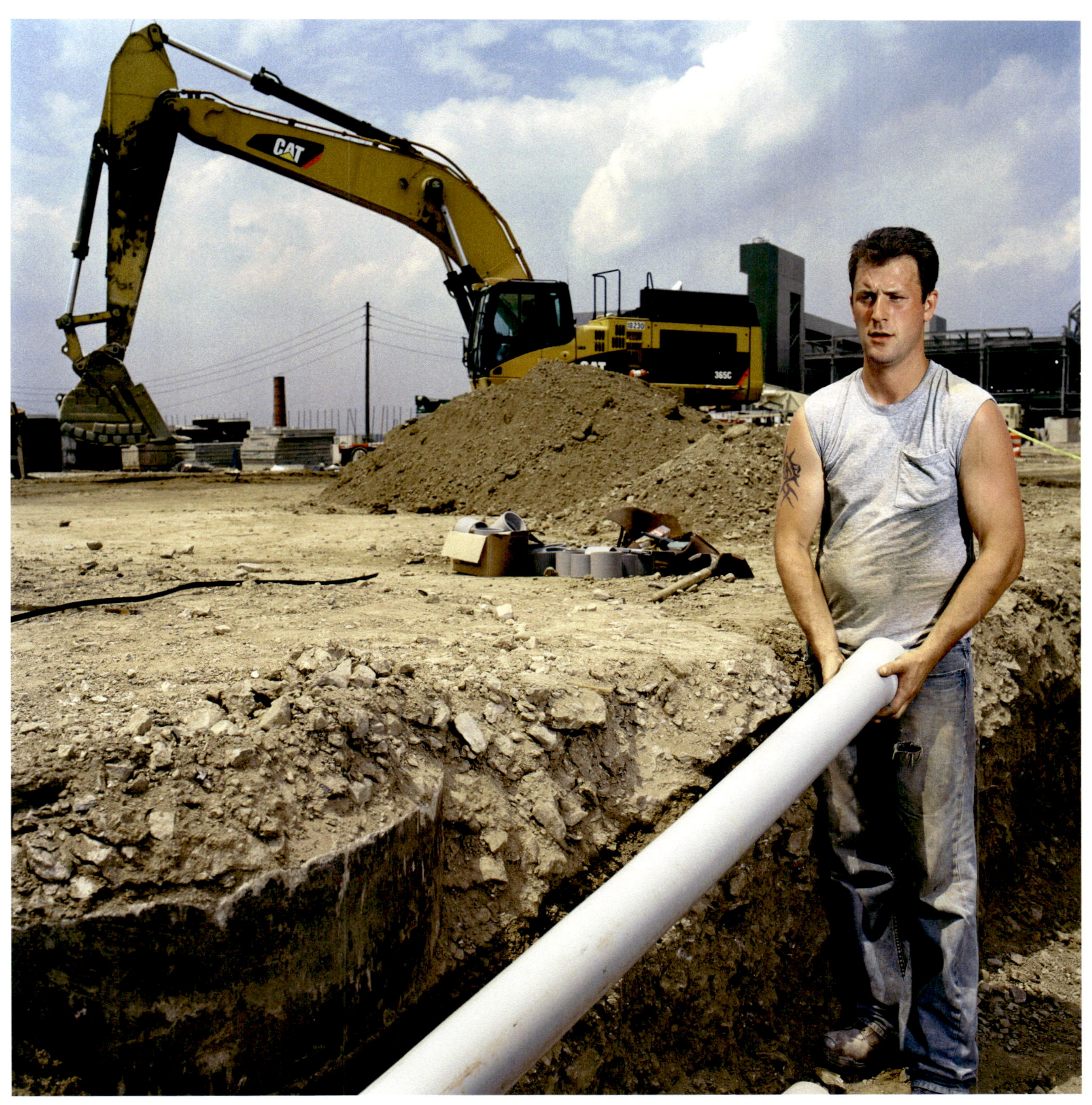

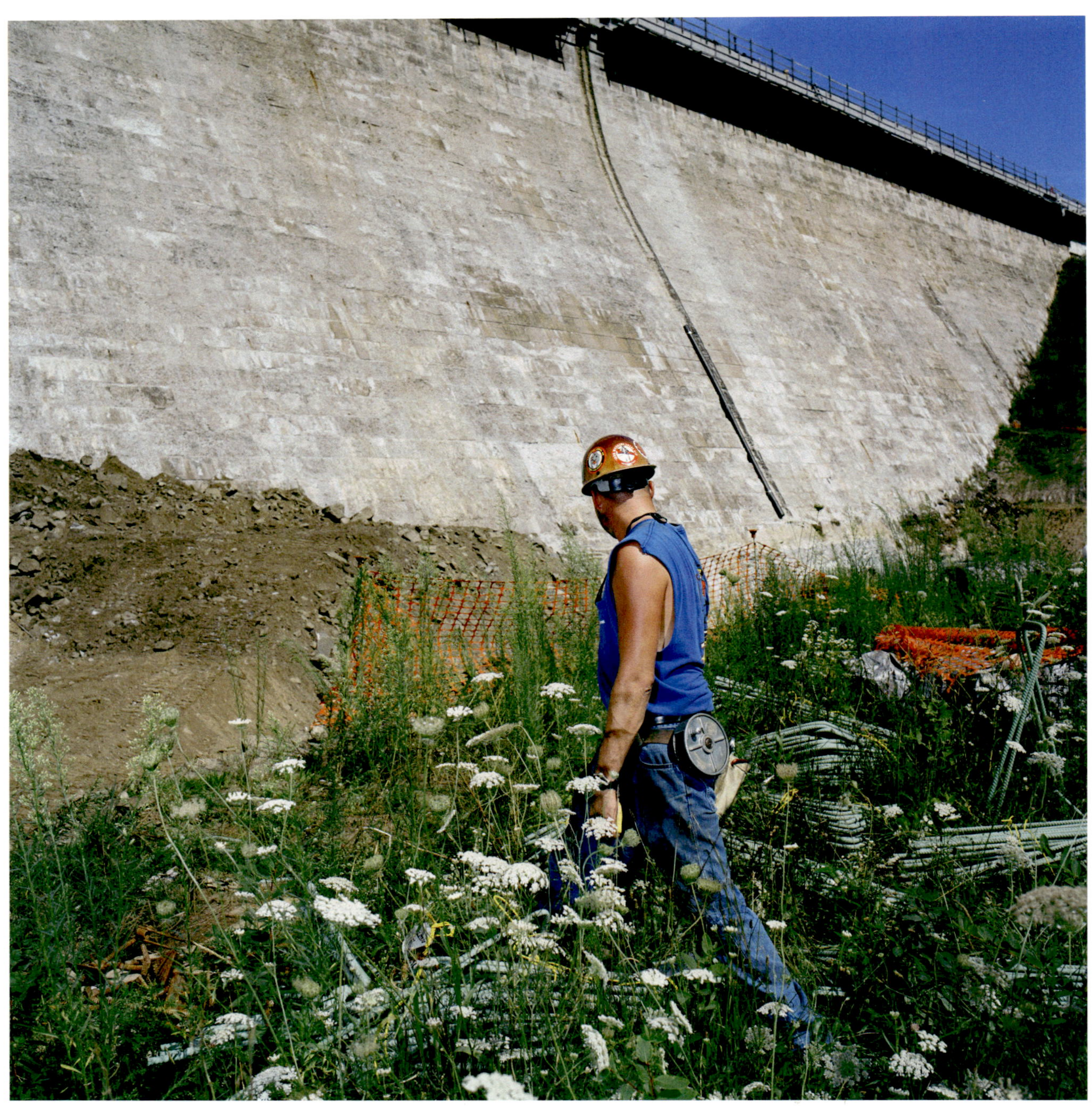

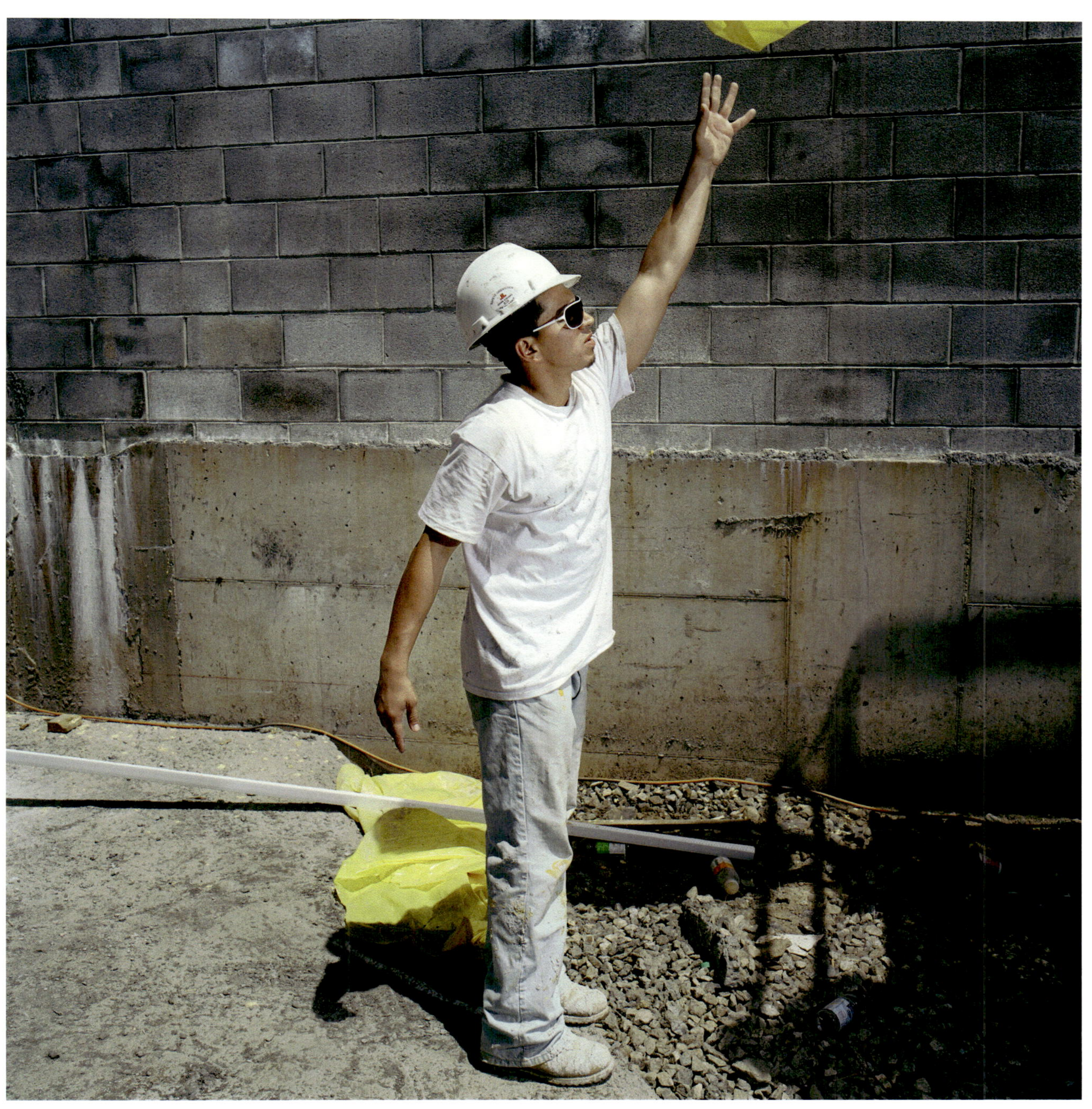

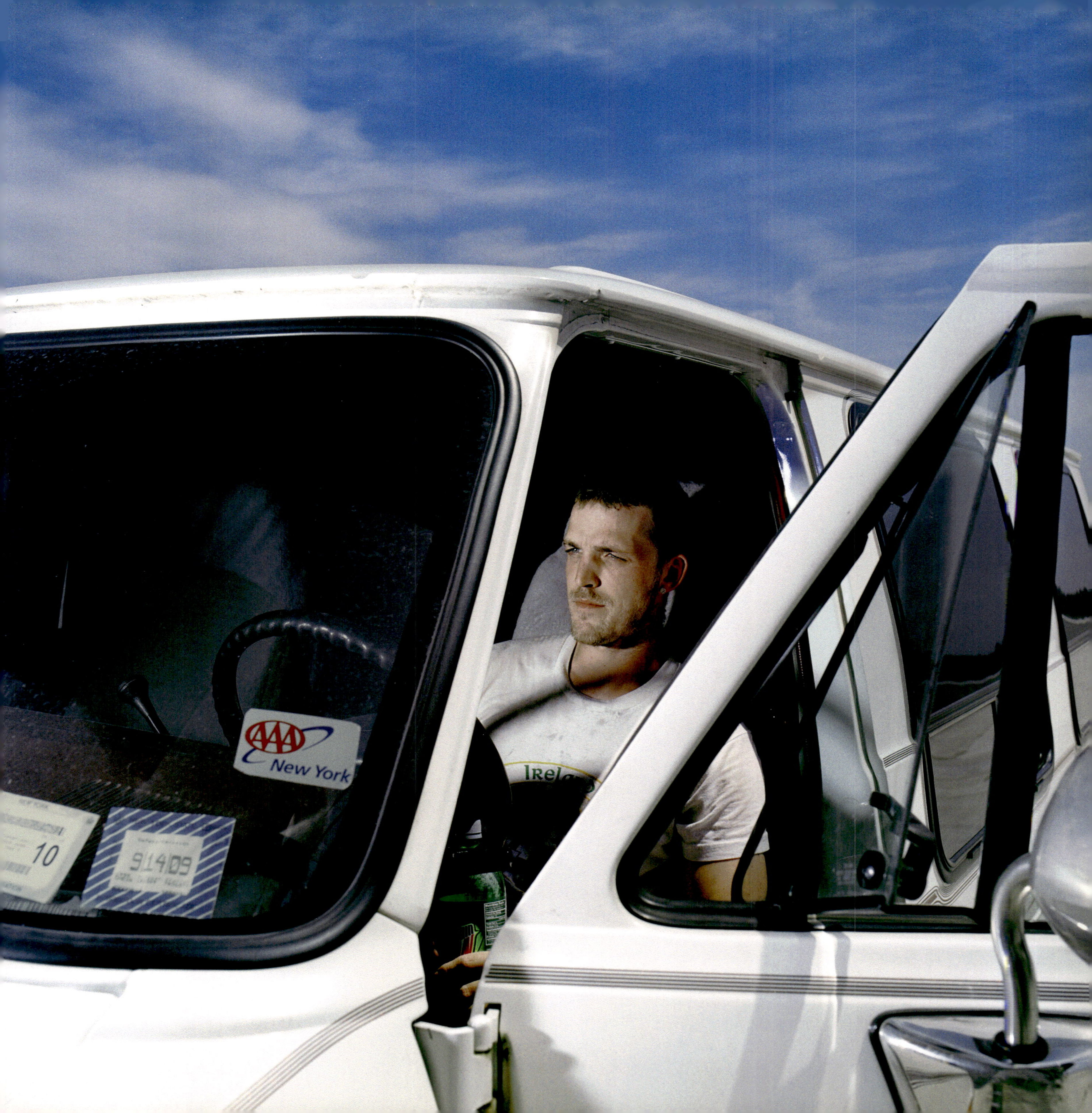
AAA
New York
10
9 14 09

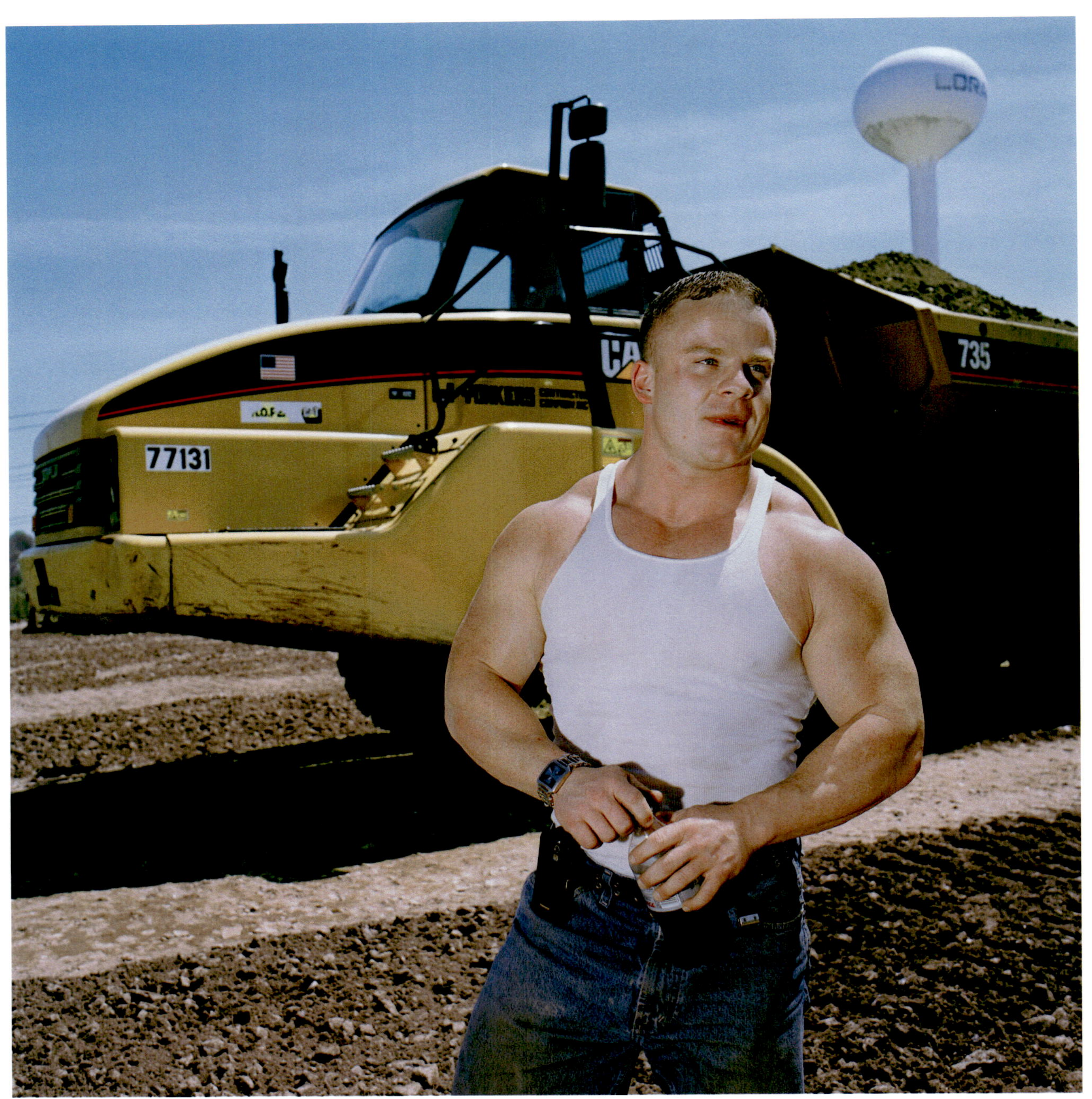

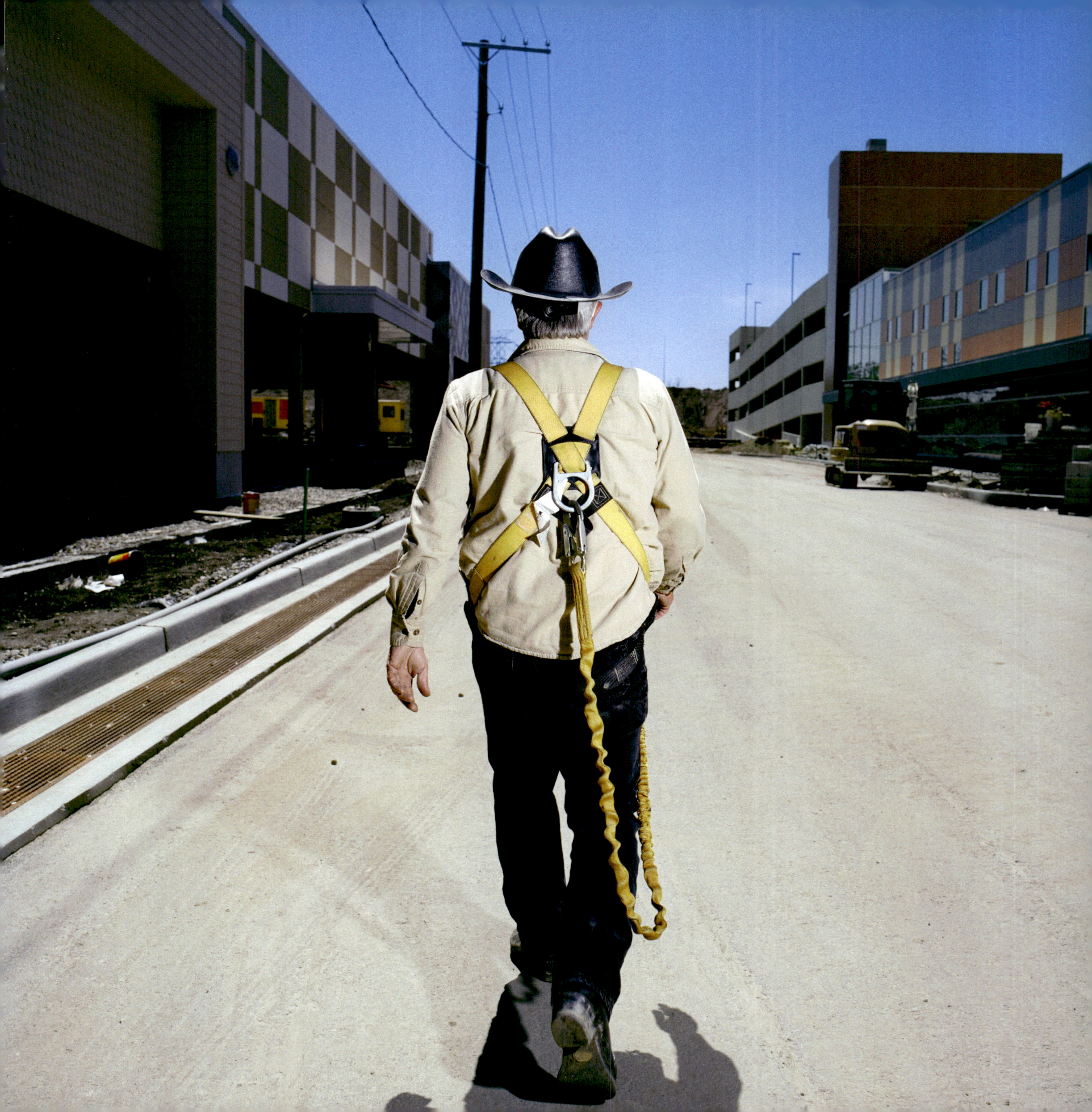

ICARUS, RECONSTRUCTED

WHITNEY JOHNSON

Eleven steelworkers, perched on an I-beam high above the Manhattan skyline, chatting and smoking cigarettes. A single figure wrapped around a cable wire, soaring high over the city. Charles C. Ebbets's *New York Construction Workers Lunching on a Crossbeam,* taken during the construction of the RCA, now GE, Building at Rockefeller Center, and Lewis Hine's *Icarus Atop the Empire State Building,* both shot in the early 1930s, are the images that emerge in our memory when we think about construction, particularly in New York City.

Photography, of course, repeats itself. So while Brian Finke sees these images as iconic, even epic, they did not serve as a starting point for his own project. For Finke, *Construction* is a continuation of earlier projects, most notably *2-4-6-8: American Cheerleaders and Football Players* and *Flight Attendants,* which began with a simple idea: to focus, obsessively, on a single group of people.

Finke's work is rooted in the documentary tradition. Early on, he was introduced to W. Eugene Smith, whose "photos and life completely blew me away, completely opened the world of social awareness." As the photographer for his high school newspaper, Finke could be found running along the sidelines of football games in the suburbs of Houston, Texas.

After art school, Finke wanted to develop his own style of documentary photography. He switched from black-and-white to color, and to the square format, adding artificial lighting to highlight his subjects and heighten reality. Perhaps more significantly, he deliberately began photographing subjects closer to home. Both of his sisters were high school cheerleaders in Texas and after living in New York City for several years Finke wanted to revisit the world of Friday Night Lights, "but without all the anxieties, or at least less of them, of being a teenager." His books, *2-4-6-8: American Cheerleaders and Football Players,* published in 2003, and *Flight Attendants,* published in 2008, showcase his new approach: a heightened documentary style that he still works within today.

Finke started his latest project at the height of the construction boom, in early 2008. In New York City, like elsewhere around the country, buildings were rising at a frenzied pace, and Finke wanted to capitalize on this energy. "I assumed there would be all this activity," Finke said. "I wanted to create images with all these visual layers."

To his surprise, Finke found something quite different at the sites, all in the greater New York City area. "It's an otherworldly place. It would feel like being out in the desert or in the middle of nowhere." And then the recession hit. "A lot of the time it was just staring at a ladder on the roof of a building, all by itself."

Finke tends to gravitate toward characters and individuals who are visually distinctive. His photographs have a way of making the person in the frame seem significant. We see this in *Construction,* perhaps most in images like the final photograph in the book of a lone cowboy walking away from us. But in a departure from his earlier work, most of his subjects, despite being front and center in the frame, merge with the landscape: the textures of their shirts, their harnesses, and the gestures of their arms all become a part of the greater scene.

In the documentary tradition, Finke's observations of this subset of society reveal something about our time. Photography may repeat itself, but these pictures are not about the drama or awe of *Icarus*. Nor are they about an architectural feat, the construction of some marvel of engineering. In fact, we are never aware of the particulars of a specific site and we never see a finished building. Instead Finke takes an honest look at what it means to be—at the daily tasks of being—a construction worker.

But for Finke, it is the act of making pictures that propels him. "Standing on a building in the middle of winter, with the New York City skyline in the background, as the steel workers heckle each other umpteen stories up from the ground—it's all kind of ridiculous and wonderful at the same time."

Whitney Johnson is the Director of Photography at The New Yorker *where she oversees the photographic vision for the print magazine, the iPad, and website, and has produced award-winning portfolios on the United States military and world leaders. She contributes regularly to the magazine's photography blog, Photo Booth, and is an adjunct professor at New York University.*

ACKNOWLEDGMENTS

Thanks to Whitney Johnson for her engaging words, John Jenkins III and DECODE Books for giving me the opportunity to publish and share this project, and Rockwell Harwood for his brilliant cover design.

Thanks to Brian Clamp for his guidance over the past eleven years, as well as his continued support.

Thanks to Hassan Sulehri for helping me begin this project and to all of the architects and builders who found the time for me to shoot.

A special thanks to all of the men and women on the job sites. They allowed me incredible access to document their work, they were patient and entertaining, and I am very grateful.

Thank you to Eric Medsker for his interpretation of the negatives. Thank you to Anthony Tafuro, Erika Engstrom, Kaz Senju, Lisa Kirshner, John Messinger, and Daniel Tepper for their assistance on sites while photographing. Thank you to Ross Kasovitz of K&M Camera for always answering the phone. And thank you to Picturehouse for producing the beautiful exhibition prints.

Thank you to my partner Lisa Daniels and to our sons Oli and Izi for their strength and encouragement.

This book is for my youngest son Izi. His fascination with construction vehicles was a strong influence in the project and I hope he can share this book with his children some day.

This first edition of *Construction* is limited to 1,500 casebound copies.

The book was designed by John Jenkins III and Rockwell Harwood.

The text is set in Formation and Eurostyle.

Photographs copyright © 2012 by Brian Finke.
Copyright © 2012 by DECODE, Inc.

Color mangement by iocolor, Seattle
Printed and bound by Shenzhen Artron Color Printing Company, LTD., China

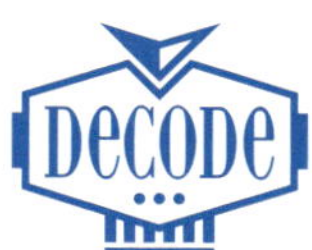

DECODE, Inc.
625 First Avenue, Suite 300
Seattle, Washington 98104
www.decodebooks.com

Available through ARTBOOK | D.A.P.
155 Sixth Avenue, 2nd Floor
New York, NY 10013
Tel: 212.627.1999 Fax: 212.627.9484

Library of Congress Control Number: 2012932882
ISBN 978-0-9833942-1-1

A special Collector's Edition consisting of a signed limited edition
photograph with a copy of *Construction* is available.
Please contact DECODE for more information: **books@decodebooks.com**